1

© John D. Travelar

TAIWAN TRAVEL
2024

A comprehensive Travel Guide for Uncovering Taiwan's History, Hidden Gems, Sightseeing also for Foodies and First-Timers

"where tradition dances with modernity, creating a harmonious tapestry of vibrant culture and boundless innovation."
TAIWAN

Book By
John D. Travelar

© John D. Travelar

Covid-19

The COVID-19 epidemic has had a severe effect on enterprises of all kinds. Many companies have been forced to shut or adjust their operational hours. As a consequence, it is crucial to check with the venue directly before coming to acquire the latest information.We have taken every attempt to verify the facts in this guide, but we suggest double-checking with the venue. Our mission is to give accurate and up-to-date information to enable our readers to make educated choices.

Here are some recommendations for verifying with the venue before visiting:

- Call the venue and inquire about their current hours of operation and any safety precautions they are following.

- Check the venue's website or social media sites for the latest information.

- If you are still undecided, it is usually advisable to err on the side of caution and wait until the situation is more stable.

We appreciate your understanding and cooperation during these tough times. We are devoted to presenting our readers with the most accurate and up-to-date information available.

© John D. Travelar

COPYRIGHT

This written content is under the umbrella of intellectual property rights, which means that duplicating or distributing it in any form, electronic, mechanical, photocopying, recording, or otherwise, without the prior written approval of the publisher, is absolutely forbidden. Any unlawful use or distribution of this guide or its components may entail serious legal penalties, and the offender will face the full power of the law.

The Taiwan Travel Guide © 2023 is the property of [**John D. TRAVELAR**], and it is covered by copyright laws and international conventions. The offender of these rights may suffer both civil and criminal consequences, as authorised by law. Therefore, we beg you to seek the publisher's express approval before any reproduction or dissemination of this information

© John D. Travelar

DISCLAIMERS

We give a disclaimer before we continue with the following travel guide, based on our own excursions and studies in Taiwan. Although we have made a genuine attempt to assure the accuracy and comprehensiveness of this guide, we cannot guarantee that all the information mentioned in this material is up-to-date or correct. It is vital to keep in mind that elements such as price, service availability, and working hours may fluctuate without prior warning.

Furthermore, this book is meant purely for instructional reasons and should not be considered as the primary source of information when making travel selections. It is always wise to perform your own study and judgement before making any trip plans or selections.

Lastly, we must notify our excellent readers that the authors and publishers of this book cannot be held liable for any loss or harm occurring from the use of this guide or the information contained within. It is the duty of the reader to check the information presented in this book before making any travel choices.

© John D. Travelar

HOW TO USE THIS GUIDE

By using this travel guide, readers acknowledge and agree to the following disclaimers and terms of use.

How to Use QR Code Maps

This guidebook includes a QR code map, which allows you to access maps, directions, and other location-specific information using your smartphone or tablet." Learn how to make the most of this useful feature:

Step 1: Prepare Your Device - Make sure you have a smartphone or tablet with a camera and internet access.

Step 2: Open Your Camera App - There is no need to take a snapshot since your camera will work as a QR code reader.

Step 3: Concentrate on the QR Code - Hold your cellphone steadily and orient it so that the QR code inside your handbook is clearly visible in the camera's perspective.

Step 4: Scan the QR Code - Your smartphone should identify the QR code immediately. When this occurs, a notice or pop-up will display. To open the link, just touch it.

Step 5: Get to the Map - You'll be sent to an interactive map or a website with detailed map directions for the area mentioned in your guidebook.

© **John D. Travelar**

Step 6: Explore and Navigate - Use the interactive map to explore the region, get directions, find areas of interest, and fully use the map instructions in your guidebook.

Step 7: Ensure Internet Connectivity - In order to load the map and get real-time information, you must have an internet connection, ideally mobile data or Wi-Fi.

Step 8: Remember that maps might change over time. If you return to the map at a later time, make sure it's accurate.

Scan Qr code

© John D. Travelar

CONTENTS

INTRODUCTION
Taiwan brief History
Overview of Taiwan
What Makes Taiwan a Special Tourist Destination

BEFORE YOU GO
Visa Requirements
Best Time to Visit
Currency and Money Tips

GETTING THERE
International Airports
Transportation within Taiwan
Language and Communication Tips

ACCOMMODATIONS
Top Hotels in Taipei
Unique Stays Across the Island
Budget-Friendly Accommodation Options

EXPLORING TAIPEI
Must-Visit Landmarks
Culinary Delights in Taipei
Shopping Hotspots

BEYOND TAIPEI
Cultural Gems in Taichung
Natural Wonders in Hualien
Historical Sites in Tainan

OUTDOOR ADVENTURES
Hiking Trails and National Parks
Water Activities and Beaches

© John D. Travelar

Cycling Routes..
TAIWANESE CUISINE..
Street Food Delights..
Regional Specialties..
Dining Etiquette...
CULTURAL EXPERIENCES.......................................
Traditional Festivals..
Temples and Religious Practices...............................
Arts and Performances..
SAFETY AND HEALTH TIPS....................................
Emergency Information...
Health Precautions..
Local Customs to Respect.......................................
SUSTAINABLE TRAVEL IN TAIWAN.........................
Eco-Friendly Initiatives...
Responsible Tourism Practices.................................
Supporting Local Communities................................
PRACTICAL TIPS...
Tipping Etiquette..
Internet and Connectivity......................................
Transportation Etiquette.......................................
SHOPPING IN TAIWAN...
Night Markets and Local Bazaars.............................
Taiwanese Souvenirs..
Bargaining Tips..
CONCLUSION...
Recap of Essential Travel Tips................................
ITINERARIES..

© John D. Travelar

INTRODUCTION

Taiwan, an East Asian treasure, has a fascinating combination of rich history, diversified culture, and technical capability. Understanding this island's rich fabric is essential for recognizing its worldwide importance. We go into the heart of Taiwan in this journey, unravelling its geographical glories, historical intricacies, cultural marvels, and the dynamic present influencing its future.

Geographical Perspectives
Taiwan, located in the western Pacific Ocean, is a region of striking contrasts. The island is a sanctuary for nature aficionados, with a diversified scenery that includes mountains, woods, and a lovely shoreline. Its strategic position has affected not just its history but also its unique wildlife.

© John D. Travelar

Background Information

The history of Taiwan is a jumble of early settlements, indigenous cultures, and foreign influences. Taiwan's history, from indigenous Austronesian peoples to Dutch and Spanish colonialism, demonstrates its tenacity and flexibility. Following Chinese administration and Japanese occupation, the island's identity was further influenced.

Taiwanese Traditions and Culture

Taiwan's cultural environment is as varied as its topography. Taiwan has a rich cultural legacy influenced by Chinese customs and indigenous behaviours. The island's culture is a dynamic tapestry that continues to grow, ranging from traditional arts and crafts to contemporary manifestations.

Development of the Economy

Taiwan has seen a dramatic economic transition in recent decades. The island's transformation from an agrarian culture to a worldwide digital powerhouse is astounding. Taiwan stands tall among economic heavyweights, with major sectors in electronics, information technology, and manufacturing.

Political Situation

Taiwan's political situation is a worldwide concern. Taiwan is a focal point in world geopolitics due to its complicated relationship with China, the island's drive for international recognition, and the delicate diplomatic dance. In today's linked globe, understanding the complexities of Taiwan's political scene is critical.

Language Varieties

© John D. Travelar

Taiwan's language variety is yet another aspect of its cultural diversity. While Mandarin is the official language, several regional dialects enrich the linguistic landscape. Language cohabitation shows the island's heterogeneous character.

Cuisine Delights

Taiwanese food is a culinary treat, a symphony of tastes and textures. Taiwan's food scene is a sensory adventure, with classic street foods like stinky tofu and culinary inventions like bubble tea. Taiwanese food is distinct and flavorful due to the blending of traditional Chinese, indigenous, and Japanese influences.

Attractions for Tourists

Taiwan is a treasure mine of experiences for tourists. From the busy night markets of Taipei to the tranquil scenery of Taroko Gorge, the island has something for everyone. Taiwan is a must-see trip because of its historical monuments, natural marvels, and contemporary icons.

Schooling System

Taiwan's education system is well-known for its quality. The island generates graduates that contribute considerably to global developments due to a high focus on academic successes. Taiwan has emerged as an educational pioneer due to its emphasis on science, technology, engineering, and mathematics (*STEM*).

Cultural Events

Taiwan's joyful mood is contagious, with a schedule jam-packed with cultural events. Each celebration has

© John D. Travelar

significant cultural importance, from the vibrant Lantern Festival to the boisterous Ghost Festival. Participating in these festivals allows you to see the core of Taiwanese culture.

Technology and Innovation

Taiwan's contribution to the global technology sector cannot be emphasised. The island, which is home to major electronics industries and a hotspot for innovation, plays a critical role in defining the future of technology. Taiwan is at the forefront of technical breakthroughs, from hardware to software.

Environmental Protection

Taiwan is cognizant of its environmental duties despite its fast expansion. The island has undertaken environmentally friendly activities, with a focus on sustainability and environmental protection. Balancing growth with environmental preservation is a major problem, and Taiwan is working hard to solve this issue.

Difficulties Overcome

Taiwan faces the problems of modernization as it navigates the twenty-first century. Balancing tradition and modernity, tackling political issues, and assuring long-term growth are all continuous efforts. Understanding these obstacles gives insight into the dynamic growth of the island.

Taiwan's future is defined by potential contributions on the global stage. Taiwan is set to continue altering the globe as a hub of innovation, keeper of cultural legacy, and participant in international affairs. The island's flexibility and resilience are the driving reasons behind its bright future. Taiwan exemplifies the healthy coexistence of tradition and modernity. Its geographical beauty, rich history, and vibrant current make it an enthralling adventure destination. Taiwan welcomes the world to observe its unique tapestry emerge as it contributes to the global story in its own unique manner.

Taiwan brief History

Inhabitants

- **Prehistoric Villages**: During Taiwan's prehistoric era, various civilizations emerged, each distinguished by sophisticated pottery, tools, and evidence of agricultural techniques. Indigenous peoples, particularly Austronesian-speaking populations, had a significant effect on the island's early history.

- **Ancient Austronesian Cultures**: Taiwan's indigenous peoples, who included ethnic groups including the Amis, Atayal, and Paiwan, had rich cultural traditions. Each group has its own language, spiritual beliefs, and creative manifestations, adding to the rich fabric of Taiwanese culture.

The Ming and Qing Dynasties

- **Colonisation by the Dutch and the Spaniards**: The Dutch and Spanish presence in Taiwan in the 17th century introduced European influence. These colonial powers participated in commerce, missionary work, and territory expansion, which led to confrontations with indigenous peoples.

- **Qing Rule and Ming Loyalists**: The effective struggle of Koxinga against the Dutch produced a short period of Ming loyalist control. However, the conquest of Taiwan by Qing Dynasty China in 1683 represented a momentous transformation, incorporating Taiwan into the Qing Empire.

Japanese Colonial Period

- **The First Sino-Japanese War, 1894-1895**: The Treaty of Shimonoseki, which handed Taiwan to Japan, was the consequence of the First Sino-Japanese War. The subsequent Japanese colonial period (1895-1945) brought industrialization, infrastructural development, and social changes.

© John D. Travelar

- **Japanese Imperial Rule (1895-1945):** Taiwan modernised under Japanese administration, but experienced obstacles such as cultural integration and labour exploitation. Some cultural components have been preserved, and a robust educational system has been established as part of the heritage.

Postwar Period

- **China Retrocession (1945):** Taiwan was returned to the Republic of China (ROC) after World War II. The ROC, commanded by the Kuomintang (KMT), assumed power, altering the political trajectory of the island.

- **Refugees from the Chinese Civil War:** Following its defeat in the Chinese Civil War by the Communist Party of China (CPC), the ROC fled to Taiwan in 1949. Taiwan was transformed into a safe haven for KMT sympathisers and mainland Chinese refugees.

The Martial Law Period

- **Authoritarian Principle:** Taiwan was ruled authoritarian for decades by Chiang Kai-shek and Chiang Ching-kuo. Martial rule was declared in 1949 and lasted until 1987. Political persecution, censorship, and restricted political liberties characterised the time.

- **Economic Wonder:** Taiwan's economic development, dubbed as the "Taiwan Miracle,"

© John D. Travelar

happened despite governmental constraints. With fast industrialization and technical developments, the island became a worldwide economic powerhouse.

Democratic Reform

- **End of Martial rule (1987):** Due to international pressure and domestic demands, martial rule was lifted in 1987, kicking off a period of political liberalisation and democracy.

- **DPP (Democratic Progressive Party):** The establishment of the DPP in 1986 signified a turn toward pro-democracy and pro-Taiwan independence politics, undermining the KMT's long-standing hegemony.

- **First Direct Presidential Election (1996):** Lee Teng-hui's election as Taiwan's first directly elected president in 1996 was a watershed moment in the island's democratic path.

Relations Across the Taiwan Strait

- **Policy of One China:** The PRC's "One-China" policy considers Taiwan to be part of its territory. Tensions over Taiwan's political status remain high, with the People's Republic of China threatening military action if Taiwan declares official independence.

17

© John D. Travelar

- **Integration of the Economy:** Despite political differences, Taiwan-China business links have developed dramatically. Cross-strait economic ties have helped Taiwan flourish, but they have also prompted worries about political reliance.

New Developments

- **Current Situation:** Taiwan maintains its independence as a self-governing democratic country with its own constitution and government. However, it confronts international hurdles as a result of PRC pressure.

- **Geopolitical Difficulties:** Taiwan's international position is complicated, with most governments refusing to recognize its sovereignty. While navigating its ties with China, the island seeks meaningful engagement in international organisations.

This brief historical review gives a detailed knowledge of Taiwan's path, from its indigenous origins to the difficulties and accomplishments of its current political scene. Each phase adds to Taiwan's distinct character and resilience.

Overview of Taiwan

Welcome to East Asia's beating heart, where the dynamic island of Taiwan beckons with a tale as varied as its

18

© John D. Travelar

environment. In this overview, we will travel across Taiwan's geographical delights, dig into its complicated history, appreciate the depth of its culture, and investigate the dynamic elements driving its present and future.

Geographical Perspectives
- Taiwan, located in the western Pacific Ocean, is a natural beauty refuge. Its varied terrain includes high mountains, lush woods, and a gorgeous shoreline that weaves a tapestry. This island, about the size of Maryland, is not only a geographical treasure but also a key trading route junction.

Historical Context
- Taiwan's history is an engrossing tale formed by early settlements, indigenous civilizations, and waves of colonialism. The island's resiliency shows through, from the Austronesian peoples to Dutch and Spanish influences. Taiwan's identity was layered by Chinese authority and Japanese occupation, resulting in a distinct combination of cultural elements.

Taiwanese Traditions and Culture
- Taiwan's cultural environment is a kaleidoscope of customs. Taiwanese culture, influenced by Chinese ancestry and indigenous beliefs, is a living monument to peace in diversity. The island celebrates a lively and changing cultural character, from traditional arts to contemporary representations.

Growth of the Economy

© John D. Travelar

- Taiwan has seen a dramatic economic transition in recent decades. The island has progressed from an agricultural civilization to a worldwide technological powerhouse, with top sectors in electronics, information technology, and manufacturing. Taiwan's economic trajectory demonstrates the country's flexibility and inventiveness.

Political Scene

- Taiwan's political situation is a worldwide concern. Taiwan is a focal point in global politics due to its delicate dance with China, quest of international recognition, and difficulties of diplomatic relations. Navigating these complexities determines the island's worldwide position.

Multilingualism

- Taiwan's linguistic variety adds another thread to the country's cultural fabric. While Mandarin is the official language, the island's linguistic diversity is enhanced by a variety of local dialects. This cohabitation demonstrates Taiwan's multicultural character and people's peace.

Gastronomic Delights

- Prepare your palate for a gourmet journey in Taiwan. Taiwanese cuisine is a combination of tastes, from classic street food like stinky tofu to the worldwide craze bubble tea. Taiwan's cuisine scene is a pleasant study of traditional Chinese, indigenous, and Japanese aspects.

Attractions for Tourists

- Taiwan is a treasure mine of adventures for the intrepid tourist. Whether visiting Taipei's busy night markets or marvelling at the natural beauty of Taroko Gorge, the island has something for everyone. Exploration of historical sights, contemporary monuments, and natural beauty awaits.

System of Education

- Taiwan's education system is well-known for its quality. The island generates graduates that contribute considerably to global developments by focusing on academic successes and a heavy emphasis on STEM subjects. Taiwan's dedication to education is a driving factor behind the country's development.

Cultural Events

- Immerse yourself in Taiwan's festive mood. The calendar is jam-packed with events, from the vibrant Lantern Festival to the lively Ghost Festival. Each event is culturally significant, offering a glimpse into the core of Taiwanese customs.

Technology and Innovation

- Taiwan has had a massive effect on the global technology sector. The island, which is home to major electronics industries and a centre for innovation, is a driving force in determining the future of technology. Taiwan continues to lead the way in technical developments, from hardware to software.

© John D. Travelar

Environmental Protection
- Taiwan is cognizant of its environmental obligations as it advances. The island has undertaken environmentally friendly programs, with a focus on sustainability and conservation. Taiwan is aggressively addressing the problem of balancing growth and environmental conservation.

Difficulties encountered
- Taiwan confronts the problems of modernization as it enters the twenty-first century. Striking a balance between tradition and modernity, negotiating political complications, and guaranteeing long-term growth are all continuous tasks. Understanding these problems allows us to better understand Taiwan's dynamic development.

Prospects for the Future
- Taiwan's future is defined by its potential global contributions. Taiwan is set to continue altering the globe as a hub of innovation, keeper of cultural legacy, and participant in international affairs. The island's flexibility and resilience are the driving reasons behind its bright future.

Taiwan welcomes the rest of the world to discover its unique combination of heritage and development. The island's tale develops in compelling ways, from its geographical beauties to a vibrant present. Taiwan's evolution leaves an unmistakable impression on the world arena, a tribute to the peaceful coexistence of its history and future.

What Makes Taiwan a Special Tourist Destination

There are many attributes and features in Taiwan that make it a special place for tourists to visit, and it is a genuinely unique tourist destination. Its unique combination of natural beauty, rich cultural legacy, and technological technologies makes it a must-see for every globetrotter looking for a varied and fulfilling experience.

1. Geographic Diversity
    - The geographical variety of Taiwan is a key appeal for visitors. The island provides a magnificent setting that appeals to a broad variety of interests, from the towering peaks of the Central Mountain variety to the

© John D. Travelar

lovely shoreline and lush flora. Nature lovers, hikers, and beachgoers will find nirvana in Taiwan.

2. Delectable Culinary Delights
- Taiwanese food is a journey in and of itself. From the famed night markets of Taipei, which provide a variety of street cuisine delights including stinky tofu, bubble tea, and oyster omelettes, to traditional Hakka delicacies in the mountainous parts, the island is a feast for the senses. The confluence of tastes represents Taiwan's gourmet scene's numerous cultural influences.

3. Extensive Culture and Festivals
- Taiwan's cultural diversity is shown by its lively festivals and customs. The yearly Lantern Festival, with its hypnotic displays of multicoloured lanterns, and the vibrant Dragon Boat Festival are just a few examples of the island's cultural tapestry. Exploring these events gives you a better knowledge of Taiwanese customs and people.

4. Technology and Innovation Hub
- Taiwan is a haven for individuals who are captivated by technology. The island, as a worldwide leader in the technology sector, is home to cutting-edge inventions and world-renowned electronics businesses. Visitors may discover the most recent technologies, marvel at technical wonders, and obtain insights into the future of innovation.

© John D. Travelar

5. Architectural and Historical Wonders
- Taiwan's architecture and historical landmarks bear witness to its rich past. The island provides a trip through time, from old temples displaying traditional Chinese style to ruins of Dutch and Japanese colonial constructions. The National Palace Museum in Taipei includes a large collection of Chinese relics that provide insight into the country's history.

6. Friendly Hospitality
- Taiwanese hospitality is well-known across the globe. Visitors often comment on the real warmth and friendliness of the inhabitants, which creates a welcoming environment for visitors. The warmth of the Taiwanese people lends an added element of pleasure to the vacation experience, whether traversing crowded marketplaces or seeking directions.

7. Reliable Public Transportation
- Taiwan's efficient and well-connected public transportation infrastructure makes exploring the country simple. Travellers can easily explore the island thanks to high-speed trains, large bus networks, and a user-friendly metro system. This ease of access enables tourists to immerse themselves in Taiwan's variety.

8. Taroko Gorge's Beautiful Landscapes
- Taroko Gorge, a must-see for environment lovers, is a beautiful gorge ornamented with marble cliffs,

25

© John D. Travelar

verdant trees, and crystal-clear rivers. Hiking routes provide an opportunity to experience the gorge's pure majesty, making it a must-see location for anyone seeking a connection with nature.

What distinguishes Taiwan as a tourist destination is its ability to smoothly combine various landscapes, rich cultural experiences, technological marvels, and friendly friendliness. The island greets visitors with open arms and promises an amazing adventure via its intriguing and complex personality.

© John D. Travelar

BEFORE YOU GO

Travelling to Taiwan offers a one-of-a-kind trip full of various encounters. Here are some important things to think about before you leave to guarantee a smooth and pleasant journey.

Visa Requirements

To guarantee a smooth entrance into this East Asian jewel, it's important to understand the visa requirements before beginning on your trip to Taiwan. This detailed guide will help you understand Taiwan's visa restrictions, whether you're planning a short visit or a prolonged stay.

1. Visa-Free Travel
    - Many visitors may enter Taiwan without a visa, making planning easier. Citizens of nearly 60

© John D. Travelar

countries, including the United States, Canada, the United Kingdom, and the majority of EU states, may remain in Taiwan for up to 90 days without a visa as of the most recent update in 2022.

2. Visitor (Tourist) Visa
- Those who are not qualified for visa-free entrance or who want to remain longer than the allotted term must apply for a Visitor Visa. Depending on your nationality, you may remain for up to 60 or 90 days with this visa. Typically, the application procedure includes submitting the necessary documentation to a Taiwanese representative office or consulate.

3. Visa Extensibility
- Taiwan offers visa extensions if you find yourself desiring to remain longer than the original time provided. It is essential to apply for a visa extension before your existing one expires. Typically, extensions are given for up to 60 days.

4. Residency Visa
- A Resident Visa is necessary for persons planning a longer stay in Taiwan for reasons such as job, education, or family reunification. The application procedure is more complicated, requiring you to provide extra documentation dependent on the purpose of your stay.

5. Work Visa

© John D. Travelar

- Taiwan provides a Working Holiday Visa to nationals of selected countries, enabling young tourists to work while seeing the country. This visa is usually available for a year and is an ideal choice for people looking for a more immersive experience in Taiwan.

6. Student Visa
- International students who want to study in Taiwan must get a Student Visa. This entails obtaining approval from a Taiwanese educational institution and submitting necessary documentation to the local representative office.

7. Visa for Professional Purposes
- A Professional Visa is required for professionals seeking work in Taiwan. This visa is often sponsored by the employer and needs Ministry of Labor clearance. It is intended for those with particular skills or knowledge.

8. Application Procedure
- Depending on the kind of visa, the application procedure differs. Filling out the application form, presenting a valid passport, passport-sized pictures, evidence of financial capabilities, trip schedule, and any extra papers appropriate to the visa category are all part of the process. It is best to apply well in advance of your intended trip date.

9. COVID-19 Factors to Consider

© John D. Travelar

- Due to the continuing worldwide epidemic, visitors visiting Taiwan may face increased COVID-19 requirements. Health declarations, quarantine procedures, and testing might all be included. Follow Taiwanese authorities' advice and stay up to date on the newest travel warnings.

10, Make Contact with Representative Offices
- If you have particular queries or need clarification on visa requirements, it is best to contact the closest Taiwanese representative office or consulate. They can give current information and advice depending on your specific situation.

Understanding Taiwan's visa regulations is an important step toward having a stress-free and pleasurable visit to this beautiful island. Whether you're a tourist, student, or professional, understanding the visa procedure improves your travel experience and sets the setting for a wonderful time in Taiwan.

Best Time to Visit

Choosing the best time to visit Taiwan is very important for a memorable trip. This guide will help you identify the optimum time to pack your bags and discover the attractions of this East Asian jewel, whether you're an outdoor enthusiast, a cultural explorer, or just looking for favourable weather.

© John D. Travelar

- **Spring (March-May)**

Spring is regarded as one of the greatest seasons to visit Taiwan. With temperatures ranging from 18 to 25 degrees Celsius (64 to 77 degrees Fahrenheit), the weather is moderate and agreeable. During this season, cherry blossoms bloom, colouring the landscapes pink and white. It's a great season for outdoor activities, cultural events, and exploring the island's rich nature.

- **Summer (June to August)**

Temperatures in the summer range from 28 to 35 degrees Celsius (82 to 95 degrees Fahrenheit). While the weather is hot and humid, it's ideal for beachgoers and water sports. During the summer months, the southern section of Taiwan, including Kenting, is famed for its stunning beaches and active nightlife. However, be prepared for typhoons on occasion, particularly in late summer.

- **Autumn (September-November)**

Another great season to visit Taiwan is in the fall. Temperatures are pleasant, ranging from 22 to 28 degrees Celsius (72 to 82 degrees Fahrenheit). Typhoons are less likely, making it an ideal time for outdoor exploration, hiking, and cultural events. The spectacular autumn foliage in locations like Alishan and Yangmingshan National Park lends another dimension of beauty to the sceneries.

© John D. Travelar

- **Winter (December to February)**

The winter season in Taiwan is the coldest, with temperatures ranging from 12 to 20 degrees Celsius (54 to 68 degrees Fahrenheit). While it may not be as cold as winter in other countries, it is an excellent season to visit the hot springs in regions such as Beitou or Wulai. Winter also brings with it joyous festivals, such as the well-known Pingxi Lantern Festival.

- **Crowds and Price Considerations**

It is critical to consider crowds and pricing in addition to the weather. Taiwan's biggest tourism season is around Chinese New Year, which occurs between January and February. Hotel and airfare prices may be higher, and popular sites may be congested at this period. Plan your vacation during the shoulder seasons of spring and autumn to avoid crowds and receive more affordable choices.

The ideal time to visit Taiwan is ultimately determined by your interests and the sort of experience you desire. Taiwan provides a broad choice of activities throughout the year, whether you're fascinated by cherry blossoms, interested in cultural events, or attracted by outdoor excursions. Consider the elements that are most important to you and organise your vacation appropriately to make the most of your stay on this magical island.

Currency and Money Tips

© John D. Travelar

Understanding the currency and successfully managing your money are essential for a pleasant travel experience in Taiwan. This book covers all you need to know about the financial environment of this East Asian location, from currency exchange to payment options.

1. Currency Fundamentals
- Taiwan's national currency is the New Taiwan Dollar (TWD), sometimes known as NT or NTD. Banknotes include denominations of 100, 500, 1,000, and 2,000, whereas coins have denominations of 1, 5, 10, 50, and 100.

2. Currency Exchange
- It is best to exchange currency at a bank, a licensed money changer, or your hotel. Airports also provide currency exchange services, albeit the prices may be less beneficial. To get the greatest value for your money, avoid unregistered street merchants while exchanging cash.

3. Credit Cards
- In cities, hotels, restaurants, and bigger establishments, credit cards are routinely accepted. Major credit cards such as Visa and MasterCard are widely accepted. Cash is generally favoured in more rural or small marketplaces. Inform your bank of your trip plans to prevent problems with card use overseas.

Withdrawals from ATMs

© John D. Travelar

- ATMs are widely available in Taiwan, particularly in cities and towns. ATMs often accept international credit and debit cards, making it easy to withdraw cash. For more interoperability, look for ATMs connected to worldwide networks such as Cirrus or PLUS.

5. Use of Cash
- While credit cards and electronic payments are often accepted, it is best to have some cash on hand, particularly when visiting smaller markets, street sellers, or rural locations. Cash is also important for public transit and some attraction admission costs.

6. Tipping Habits
- Tipping is not a prevalent practice in Taiwan, and it is often not expected. Exceptional service is often recognized with a simple thank you. In certain upmarket restaurants, the bill may contain a 10% service fee.

7. Bargaining and bargaining
- Bargaining is not frequent in established businesses or marketplaces, although it may be acceptable in less formal contexts, such as street markets. Politeness is crucial, as is being courteous throughout any talks.

8. Costs and Budgeting
- Taiwan is often thought to be inexpensive for tourists. Create a daily budget that includes accommodations, food, transportation, and activities. Prices vary

© John D. Travelar

depending on location, with cities being somewhat more costly than rural locations.

9. Mobile Payments
- Taiwan is at the cutting edge of mobile payment technology. Apple Pay, Google Pay, and local solutions such as EasyCard and iPass are widely accepted. Linking your credit or debit card to these mobile payment services makes your purchases more convenient.

10. Precautions and Safety
- When handling money, use caution, particularly in busy areas. When counting cash, use reputed ATMs and be discreet. Notify your bank of your trip intentions to prevent any possible card use concerns.

11. Currency Converter Apps
- Install a currency conversion software on your smartphone to effortlessly convert TWD pricing to your local currency. This allows you to make more educated judgments whether buying or eating.

12. Refunds of Taxes
- Tourists in Taiwan are entitled to a VAT refund if their purchases surpass a specified threshold. Keep your receipts and ask participating shops about the VAT refund procedure.

© **John D. Travelar**

Navigating Taiwan's currency and money situation is critical to having a stress-free vacation experience. You'll be well-equipped to make the most of your financial transactions throughout your stay in this exciting location if you grasp the local currency, embrace a range of payment options, and follow these vital suggestions.

© John D. Travelar

GETTING THERE

The first step in creating a smooth travel experience is navigating the logistics of getting there. This book contains vital information on transit alternatives, entrance ports, and travel suggestions for Taiwan.

International Airports

The International airports serve an important role in greeting people from all over the globe as a gateway to Taiwan's various landscapes and rich culture. This resource contains vital information about Taiwan's main international airports, including facility information, transit alternatives, and arrival and departure recommendations.

© John D. Travelar

Taiwan Taoyuan International Airport (TPE)

Taiwan Taoyuan International Airport, located around 40 kilometres west of Taipei, serves as the island's principal international gateway. TPE, being one of Asia's busiest airports, provides a broad variety of services and facilities to passengers. Key characteristics include:

- **Terminology**: Terminal 1 and Terminal 2 are the two terminals at TPE. Immigration, customs, and baggage claim services are available at each terminal.
- **Transportation**: Several modes of transportation link the airport to Taipei and other places of Taiwan. High-speed trains, buses, taxis, and airport shuttles are all handy modes of transportation.

- **Aviation**: TPE is a hub for major Taiwanese airlines such as China Airlines and EVA Air. In addition, various foreign airlines fly to and from TPE.

- **Products and Services**: The airport has several amenities, including lounges, duty-free shopping, currency exchange, and medical facilities.

Songshan Airport

Songshan Airport, located in Taipei City, operates as a secondary international airport, handling both domestic and limited international flights. Songshan Airport's key features include:

© John D. Travelar

- **Address**: Songshan Airport, located closer to Taipei's city centre than Taoyuan International Airport, provides convenience for guests staying in Taipei.

- **Internal Flights**: While Songshan mostly serves internal flights, it also serves foreign destinations in Japan, South Korea, and China.

- **Transportation**: Songshan Airport is easily accessible, with choices including buses, taxis, and the Taipei Metro.
- **Aviation**: Songshan Airport serves as a hub for local flights as well as foreign airlines such as Japan Airlines.

Additional International Airports

While Taoyuan and Songshan are the main international airports, Taiwan has many more airports that handle minor foreign flights. Among the most notable are:

- **International Airport of Kaohsiung (KHH):** Kaohsiung International Airport, located in southern Taiwan, acts as a regional gateway and provides international flights to a variety of locations.

- **RMQ (Taichung International Airport):** Taichung International Airport, located in central Taiwan, runs certain international flights, making it convenient for visitors to the island.

© John D. Travelar

International Arrival Travel Tips

- **Visa processes**: Before arriving in Taiwan, make sure you have completed all appropriate visa processes depending on your nationality and the purpose of your visit.

- **Declarations of Customs**: To ensure a seamless customs declaration procedure upon arrival, familiarise yourself with Taiwan's customs rules.

- **Transportation Options**: Research and schedule your transportation to and from the airport. Whether travelling by high-speed rail, bus, or cab, having a plan in place assures a smooth trip.

- **Language Support**: While English is commonly recognized, knowing certain words in Mandarin may be useful, particularly when conversing with taxi drivers or requesting assistance.

Considerations for Departure

- **Check-in formalities**: Arrive early at the airport to complete check-in formalities. Many foreign flights leaving Taiwan allow for online check-in, which adds convenience.

- **Security Check**: Prepare for security screening processes, including passport and ticket inspections. To speed up the procedure, familiarise yourself with the rules.

© John D. Travelar

- **Free Duty Shopping**: Duty-free shopping is available at airports. Taiwan's international airports sell everything from local specialties to worldwide brands.

Navigating Taiwan's international airports is the first step in exploring the island's beauty and culture. Whether you arrive at Taoyuan International Airport or Songshan Airport, the facilities and services offered guarantee a seamless and delightful travel experience from the time you arrive.

Transportation within Taiwan

Exploring Taiwan's bustling cities, gorgeous landscapes, and cultural treasures becomes an exciting journey once you arrive. Understanding Taiwan's many transportation alternatives is critical for smooth and comfortable travel. This guide will help you travel the island by providing information on the main types of transportation.

HSR (High-Speed Rail)

Taiwan's High-Speed Rail (HSR) is a contemporary transportation wonder, linking major cities at breakneck speeds. The HSR's key characteristics are as follows:

- **Efficiency and Speed**: The HSR can move at up to 300 km/h (186 mph), making it the quickest method

© John D. Travelar

to travel between cities such as Taipei, Taichung, Tainan, and Kaohsiung.

- **Availability**: The HSR, with its strategically placed stops, enables easy access to city cores and important attractions.

- **Comfort**: Spacious, comfy chairs and well-designed stations contribute to a pleasurable journey.

Trains and Local Rail Services

Aside from the HSR, Taiwan has a large network of classical trains and local rail services. Highlights of Taiwanese rail travel include:

- **Nature Routes**: Certain lines, particularly those along the east coast and across hilly areas, provide stunning scenery, making rail travel a pleasant experience.

- **Local discovery**: Smaller towns and cities are connected by local train services, allowing for immersive discovery of Taiwan's different areas.

- **Recurring Departures**: Train travel is a versatile alternative for people who wish to explore at their own leisure, thanks to frequent departures.

© John D. Travelar

Intercity Coaches and Buses

Buses and intercity coaches are dependable and cost-effective forms of transportation in Taiwan. Here's what you should know:

- **Large Network**: Buses travel short and large distances, linking cities, suburbs, and even isolated locales.

- **Cost Effectiveness**: Bus travel is inexpensive, making it a good alternative for those trying to save money on transportation.

- **Affordability**: Longer travels are made more pleasurable by intercity coaches' plush seats and facilities.

The Taipei Metro and the Kaohsiung MRT

The Taipei Metro and the Kaohsiung MRT are both effective rapid transport systems that serve their respective metropolitan regions. Key characteristics include:

- **Availability**: These metro lines give fast and easy access to famous Taipei and Kaohsiung locations.

- **Smart Cards**: Rechargeable smart cards EasyCard and iPass ease payment for metro journeys and can also be used on buses and for minor transactions.

- **Secure and Clean**: The cleanliness, safety, and user-friendliness of the Taipei Metro and Kaohsiung MRT are well-known.

Taxis and Ride-Hailing Apps

Taxis and ride-sharing applications provide door-to-door service, which is particularly useful in places with limited public transit. Take a look at the following:

- **Taxis with Metres**: Taxis are widely accessible in cities, and most drivers utilise metres to calculate clear fares.

- **Ride-Sharing Applications**: Uber and other local alternatives give another choice for quick and dependable transportation.

Renting a Car or a Scooter

Renting a vehicle or scooter is an appealing option for people seeking flexibility and freedom. Take a look at the following:

- **Leisure to Explore**: Having your own car enables you to visit off-the-beaten-path locations and take unexpected diversions.

- **Road Situation**: Taiwan's roads are well-maintained, however traffic in cities may be congested, and driving demands prudence.

© John D. Travelar

- **Culture of the Scooter:** Scooters are a common means of transportation, particularly in cities. A scooter rental is a unique opportunity to explore local life.

Bike Shares and Cycling

Cycling and bike sharing give an alternate method to experience Taiwan for the environmentally aware tourist. The following are some key points:

- **Bike Trails**: Cycling is a fun and ecologically responsible choice in many cities and attractive locations that have dedicated bike routes.

- **Bike Share Programs**: Cities such as Taipei and Kaohsiung have public bike-sharing schemes that enable you to borrow and return bikes at a variety of places.

Domestic Flights and Ferries

Exploring Taiwan's outlying islands and isolated locations may need the use of boats or domestic planes. Take a look at the following:

- **Island Hopping**: Ferries link the main island with outlying islands such as Penghu, Kinmen, and Matsu, each of which offers a distinct cultural experience.

- **Internal Flights**: Domestic flights are a fast and effective way to get to more distant places.

© John D. Travelar

Using Taiwan's transportation alternatives combines contemporary efficiency with traditional charm. The numerous alternatives suit every traveller's interests, whether you're speeding between towns on the HSR, visiting local markets by bus, or drifting along picturesque routes on a rental scooter.

FAQs

- 1. How can I buy High-Speed Rail (HSR) tickets in Taiwan? Tickets for the HSR may be bought at the station, online, or via mobile applications. Booking ahead of time is advised, particularly during high travel periods.
- 2. Are taxis easily accessible in Taiwan? Yes, cabs are widely accessible in cities, and hailing one is typically simple. The majority of drivers use metres to calculate their fares.

- 3. Can I use the same EasyCard or iPass for both the metro and buses in Taipei? Yes, both the EasyCard and the iPass may be used on the Taipei Metro, buses, and other kinds of public transit, allowing for a quick and smooth payment experience.

- 4. Do Taiwan's cities have dedicated bike paths? Yes, many Taiwanese cities have dedicated bike routes, making riding a safe and pleasurable way to explore cities.

© John D. Travelar

- 5. How do I go to remote islands like Penghu or Kinmen?To reach remote islands like Penghu or Kinmen, the principal forms of transportation are ferries and domestic planes. Domestic flights are accessible from major airports, and ferries leave from particular ports.

Language and Communication Tips

Travelling to Taiwan is not only a feast for the senses, but it is also a chance to participate with the local culture. Despite the fact that Mandarin is the official language, navigating the linguistic terrain requires a few language and communication strategies. This book seeks to improve your communication skills, build relationships, and enrich your Taiwan travel experience.

- **Understand Basic Mandarin Phrases**

While many people in cities and tourist regions understand English, learning a few basic Mandarin phrases will help you get by. Simple greetings, thank expressions, and simple queries may break the ice and win you smiles from locals. Consider learning words such as "Ni hao" (Hello), "Xie xie" (Thank you), and "Zai jian" (Farewell).

- **Make Use of Translation Apps**

Translation applications might be your language buddies in this digital era. Apps like Google Translate or local versions may assist you with understanding signs, menus, and engaging in basic discussions. Downloading an offline version

© John D. Travelar

might be useful, particularly in locations with restricted internet access.

• Make Use of Body Language and Gestures

Nonverbal communication is an international language. Use gestures and body language to communicate your message. A grin, nod, or simple hand gestures may frequently transcend the language divide and successfully explain your intentions.

• English in Cities

English is frequently spoken in large cities including Taipei and Kaohsiung, particularly at tourist-friendly enterprises, hotels, and transit hubs. Feel comfortable conversing in English, although a courteous try in Mandarin is always welcome.

• Pay Attention to Local Pronunciations

Pay attention to tones while practising Mandarin sentences. Mandarin is a tonal language, therefore the meaning of a word might alter depending on your voice pitch. While most locals are tolerant of non-native speakers, making an effort to pronounce words properly shows respect for the language.

• Use Language Apps for Cultural Understanding

Language applications may do more than just translate; they can also provide cultural context. HelloTalk apps link you with native speakers for language interaction, allowing you to learn about local customs and traditions and get individual language suggestions.

• Be Patient and Mindful

© John D. Travelar

Cultural and linguistic diversity are an inherent element of the travel experience. Be patient, open-minded, and eager to learn in your encounters. Locals value visitors who are genuinely interested in their culture and language.

- **Make liberal use of polite phrases**

In every culture, politeness goes a long way. Use words like "Qing wen" (Excuse me), "Bu hao yi si" (Sorry), and "Dui bu qi" (I'm sorry) in your conversations. In Taiwanese culture, politeness is highly prized.

- **Participate in Local Language Experiences**

Participating in local activities such as culinary lessons, cultural events, or language meetups offers a rich setting for language practice. Interacting with locals in a casual situation may help you improve your conversational abilities.

- **Respect Local Addressing Customs**

In Taiwan, persons are often addressed by their title and last name, followed by titles such as "Xian Sheng" (Mr.), "Nu Shi" (Mrs.), or "Xiao Jie" (Miss). Respect is shown by correct speech in Taiwanese culture.

- **Pay Attention to Local Dialects**

While Mandarin is the official language, local dialects may exist in certain areas. Recognizing this and modifying your linguistic style appropriately demonstrates cultural awareness.

Navigating Taiwan's linguistic terrain will enhance your vacation experience. Whether you're learning Mandarin phrases, utilising translation apps, or participating in local

© John D. Travelar

activities, adopting the language and communication guidelines described in this book can strengthen your connection with Taiwan's people and culture.

© John D. Travelar

ACCOMMODATIONS

Choosing the correct hotel is an important part of any trip experience, and Taiwan has a wide range of alternatives to meet any traveller's interests. This book gives insights into Taiwan's lodging delights, from contemporary hotels to traditional guesthouses, assuring a pleasant and enjoyable stay.

Modern Hotels in Urban Retreats
Taiwan's cities are home to a multitude of contemporary hotels catering to a wide range of budgets and interests. Among the highlights are:

- **Luxury Accommodations:** Internationally recognized hotel chains provide opulent rooms with first-rate amenities, spa services, and panoramic city views.

© John D. Travelar

- **Boutique** Hotels: Quaint boutique hotels provide a distinct combination of comfort and flair, and are often situated in hip areas.

- **Hotels for Business:** Business hotels that are well-equipped cater to the demands of business visitors by providing accessible locations and important facilities.

Cultural Immersion at Traditional Guesthouses

Consider staying at a traditional guesthouse, particularly in rural or historic places, for a more immersive experience. Key characteristics include:

- **Cultural Atmosphere**: Guesthouses often include native architecture and design, enabling visitors to get immersed in Taiwan's rich cultural legacy.

- **Individualised Service**: Smaller businesses provide individualised service, with hosts often giving insights on local customs, traditions, and hidden treasures.

- **Community Relationship**: Some guesthouses are located in small settlements, allowing visitors to interact with people and experience true everyday life.

Hostels for Low-Cost Adventures

© John D. Travelar

Hostels in Taiwan are an excellent choice for budget tourists. Take a look at the following:

- **Dormitory Style:** Hostels often provide dormitory-style lodgings, creating a sociable environment for visitors to meet.

- **Common spaces**: The hostel's common spaces, shared kitchens, and planned events provide a dynamic and sociable atmosphere.

- **Convenient Locations**: Many hostels are ideally positioned in the centre of cities or near renowned tourist sites, making them ideal for sightseeing.

Relaxing Hot Spring Resorts

Taiwan is famous for its hot springs, and vacationing in a hot spring resort is a one-of-a-kind and refreshing experience. Among the highlights are:

- Natural Preferences: Natural hot springs surrounded by gorgeous scenery are often included in resorts, providing a tranquil and soothing mood.

- Spa Services: Aside from hot springs, several resorts include spa services, massages, and wellness treatments for a more comprehensive stay.

- Culinary Delights: Enjoy local and foreign cuisine in on-site restaurants, which complements the whole leisure experience.

Airbnb Listings for Local Homestays

Consider arranging a local homestay via Airbnb for a more customised touch. Among the advantages are:

- **Local Perspectives**: Hosts may give important local knowledge by recommending off-the-beaten-path sites and eating options.

- **Home Comforts**: Enjoy the amenities of a home away from home, including private rooms, communal areas, and the ability to interact with local hosts.

- **Variety of Options**: Airbnb offerings span from city apartments to rural cottages, providing a broad selection of options for any tourist.

Environmentally Friendly Accommodations for Sustainable Travel

If environmental sustainability is important to you, Taiwan provides eco-friendly lodging alternatives. Take a look at the following:

- **Green Initiatives**: Sustainable methods such as energy saving, trash reduction, and community involvement are prioritised in eco-friendly hotels.

- **Proximity to Nature**: Some environmentally friendly solutions are tucked in natural settings, giving a relaxing escape while reducing environmental effects.

© John D. Travelar

- **Cultural Preservation**: Certain lodgings concentrate on conserving local culture and customs, therefore contributing to community sustainability.

Tips for Booking Accommodation in Taiwan
- **Address**: Choose your lodgings depending on your itinerary. Consider the neighbourhood's closeness to attractions, public transit, and general atmosphere.

- **Comments and Ratings**: Examine online reviews and ratings on platforms such as TripAdvisor or booking websites to learn about prior guests' experiences.

- **Reservation Platforms**: To get the greatest discounts, use popular booking sites. Booking.com, Agoda, and Airbnb provide a broad choice of possibilities.

- **Cultural Awareness**: Respect local norms and regulations, particularly while staying in traditional lodgings. Learn proper manners, such as removing your shoes in specific situations.

Top Hotels in Taipei

Taipei, Taiwan's lively capital, provides a fascinating combination of technology and culture, and finding the perfect lodging is critical for a great trip. This directory reveals Taipei's greatest hotels, from opulent worldwide

© John D. Travelar

chains to boutique gems, offering a perfect balance of comfort and refinement.

Shangri-La's Far Eastern Plaza Hotel in Taipei

- **Address**: No. 201, Dunhua South Road, Da'an District

Shangri-La's Far Eastern Plaza Hotel dominates the Taipei skyline. This five-star hotel is a favourite among discriminating guests, with panoramic city views and opulent facilities. Among the highlights are:

- **Exquisite Dining**: Indulge in culinary pleasures at the hotel's award-winning restaurants, which serve a variety of foreign and regional cuisines.

- **Pool of Infinity**: The rooftop infinity pool offers a tranquil respite with stunning views of Taipei 101, offering the ideal hideaway in the centre of the city.

- **Exquisite Accommodations**: The spacious rooms and suites include modern decor, luxurious furniture, and modern comforts to provide a relaxing stay.

Mandarin Oriental, Taipei

- **Address**: 158 Dunhua North Road, Songshan District

Mandarin Oriental, Taipei, expertly blends luxury and classic elegance. This five-star hotel is well-known for its

56

© John D. Travelar

outstanding service and attention to detail. Key characteristics include:

- **Wellness and Spa**: The hotel's spa is a serene haven, providing a variety of holistic treatments and wellness programs to revitalise mind and body.

- **Michelin-Starred Dining**: Indulge in culinary perfection at Michelin-starred restaurants, which provide a fusion of foreign and traditional Taiwanese cuisines.

- **Exquisite Design**: Elegant decor and well collected artworks create a sophisticated environment, offering a sumptuous refuge in the centre of Taipei.

W Taipei

- **Address**: No. 10, Zhongxiao East Road, Xinyi District

W Taipei is a vibrant and fashionable hotel that represents the vitality of modern Taipei. W Taipei is popular among trend setters because of its cutting-edge design and energetic environment. Among the highlights are:

- **Modern Rooftop Bar**: The WOOBAR on the rooftop is a trendy spot for drinks and panoramic city views, particularly around dusk.

- **Modern Accommodations**: The rooms and suites are created with a modern flare, with modern art and facilities that appeal to the demands of the modern tourist.

- **Convenient Location**: W Taipei, located in the popular Xinyi District, provides easy access to shopping, entertainment, and Taipei 101.

Grand Hyatt Taipei

- **Address**: 2 Songshou Road, Xinyi District

The Grand Hyatt Taipei is a magnificent refuge in the middle of the city, situated near to Taipei 101. It provides a sophisticated experience and is known for its exquisite architecture and great hospitality. Among the notable characteristics are:

- **Oasis Club Spa**: The spa offers a tranquil retreat with a variety of treatments, an outdoor pool, and a fitness centre, guaranteeing clients reach the pinnacle of relaxation.

- **A Variety of Dining Options**: From traditional steakhouses to genuine Cantonese cuisine, Grand Hyatt Taipei has something for everyone's taste.

© John D. Travelar

- **Luxurious Event Locations**: The hotel's event facilities, which combine utility and elegant aesthetics, are suitable for business conventions and social gatherings.

Regent Taipei

- **Address**: 3 Lane 39, Section 2, Zhongshan North Road

The Regent Taipei is a noteworthy hotel that combines traditional grandeur with contemporary refinement. It is a popular option for both business and leisure tourists because of its central location and attention to detail. Among the notable characteristics are:

- **Gourmet Dining:** Indulge in fine dining experiences at restaurants such as Mihan Honke and Silks House, where culinary artistry takes centre stage.

- **Arcade Shopping**: The hotel has a carefully chosen mix of high-end shops and designer outlets, offering a one-of-a-kind shopping experience on the grounds.

- **Fine Spa**: The Wellspring Spa provides a variety of revitalising treatments that blend old healing traditions with current health practices.

Choosing a hotel in Taipei is more than simply a place to stay; it's about immersing yourself in the lively energy and culture of the city. Whatever hotel you like, be it Shangri-La's

© John D. Travelar

contemporary elegance or W Taipei's trendy atmosphere, these best hotels promise an amazing stay in the heart of Taiwan's city.

FAQs

- 1. Do I need to reserve accommodations in Taipei ahead of time? While Taipei provides a variety of hotels, it is best to plan ahead of time, particularly during busy tourist seasons or major events.

- 2. Do these hotels provide airport transportation? Many premium hotels in Taipei provide airport transportation. It is best to verify with the hotel ahead of time or to organise transportation independently.

- 3. Are these hotels appropriate for business travellers? Yes, many hotels appeal to business visitors by providing services such as conference rooms, business centres, and handy positions in business areas.

- 4. Do these hotels provide vegetarian or vegan dining options? Yes, these hotels often accommodate a variety of dietary preferences. Guests may request vegetarian or vegan alternatives while eating out.

- 5. Do these hotels provide tour or excursion services to their guests? Many luxury hotels in Taipei include concierge services that may help visitors arrange tours, excursions, and transportation to explore the city and its surroundings.

© John D. Travelar

Unique Stays Across the Island

These unique lodgings, ranging from mountain getaways to seaside hideaways, enrich your vacation experience by giving a look into the island's beauty and warmth.

Maokong Tea Plantation Homestays

- The address is Maokong, Wenshan District, Taipei

Get away from the hustle and bustle of the city and immerse yourself in the serene environment of Maokong, noted for its tea plantations. Homestays hidden in the lush hills provide:

- **Tea Culture Immersion**: Learn the technique of tea-making from picking leaves to creating the perfect cup firsthand. Homestay hosts often share their knowledge and enthusiasm for tea culture.

- **Views from Above:** Wake up to spectacular views of the tea terraces and the city below. Enjoy the tranquillity of nature yet just a short distance from Taipei's metropolitan core.

- **Local food:** Indulge in traditional Taiwanese food, with many homestays serving meals produced from locally sourced ingredients, giving visitors a true experience of the area.

© John D. Travelar

Alishan Treehouse Retreats

The beautiful woods and spectacular dawn views of Alishan set the backdrop for a memorable stay in quaint treehouses. Among the features are:

- **Explore Nature**: Stay in a treehouse amid old cypress trees, surrounded by nature's noises. Alishan's tranquil atmosphere provides a relaxing escape.

- **Sunrise Adventure**: Get up early to see the spectacular Alishan sunrise. Treehouses provide an excellent vantage point for seeing the sun's first rays illuminate the magnificent countryside.

- **Cultural Discovery**: Alishan has a thriving indigenous culture. Many treehouse lodgings include traditional aspects, enabling visitors to engage with the local culture.

Beitou Hot Spring Villas

- Address: Beitou, Taipei

Beitou, known for its geothermal hot springs, has exquisite hot spring villas that provide a unique combination of relaxation and enjoyment. Among the highlights are:

- **Private Hot Springs**: In the solitude of your villa, enjoy the therapeutic benefits of mineral-rich hot springs. Open-air baths with breathtaking views are available in certain lodgings.

© John D. Travelar

- **Zen Gardens**: Many hot spring homes are built within beautifully planted gardens, resulting in a Zen-like setting that compliments the relaxing hot spring experience.

- **Cuisine Delights**: Gourmet dining alternatives allow you to explore the local culinary scene. Some villas provide traditional Taiwanese cuisine, adding to the entire cultural experience.

Tamsui Fisherman's Wharf Lighthouses

Consider staying in a lighthouse-themed lodging near Tamsui's Fisherman's Wharf for a seaside retreat with a touch of nautical flair. Among the features are:

- **Nautical Atmosphere**: With nautical-themed design and architecture, experience the feel of a lighthouse. Some hotels provide spectacular ocean views.

- **Romance by the Sea:** Take leisurely strolls along the scenic Lover's Bridge and explore the bustling ambiance of Fisherman's Wharf.

- **Fresh Seafood**: Tamsui is well-known for its fresh fish. Stay in a lighthouse-themed hotel and dine on freshly caught seafood from neighbouring markets and restaurants.

© John D. Travelar

Wulai Indigenous Tribe Lodges

- **Address**: Wulai, New Taipei City

Wulai, home of the Atayal indigenous people, offers a one-of-a-kind chance to stay in traditional lodges and learn about indigenous culture. The following are important considerations:

- Cultural Immersion: Integrate into the Atayal community by taking part in cultural events, traditional rituals, and learning about the tribe's history and traditions.

- Natural Mode: Wulai is surrounded by lush woods, hot springs, and picturesque scenery. Lodges often merge harmoniously with nature, providing a tranquil and immersive experience.

- Local Handicrafts: Support local craftsmen by buying handcrafted crafts and traditional Atayal goods, which helps to create a meaningful relationship with the indigenous population.

Taiwan's one-of-a-kind accommodations offer a magical touch to your tour, enabling you to interact with the island's different landscapes and cultures. Be it's drinking tea on the slopes of Maokong, waking up in an Alishan treehouse, or immersing yourself in Wulai customs, these accommodations provide an amazing experience.

© John D. Travelar

FAQs

- 1. Is it possible to reserve a tea plantation homestay in Maokong without making previous arrangements? While some homestays accept walk-ins, it is best to book ahead of time, particularly during high seasons, to reserve your desired dates and guarantee a smooth experience.

- 2. Are Beitou hot spring villas ideal for families? Many Beitou hot spring villas cater to families, with family-friendly amenities and private hot spring facilities for a pleasant and pleasurable stay.

- 3. Can I readily explore the environs of Fisherman's Wharf from my lighthouse-themed Tamsui accommodations? Yes, lighthouse-themed hotels at Tamsui's Fisherman's Wharf allow easy access to the waterfront, Lover's Bridge, and local attractions on foot.

- 4. Are Wulai's indigenous tribal lodges accessible to single travellers? Yes, indigenous tribal lodges in Wulai are often available to solitary visitors, offering cultural immersion and a one-of-a-kind experience in a natural and social environment.

- 5. Do I need to bring cash with me while staying at these unusual accommodations? While major credit cards are frequently accepted, having some cash on hand is recommended, particularly when touring local

© John D. Travelar

markets, eating at smaller restaurants, or taking part in cultural events.

Budget-Friendly Accommodation Options

Travelling on a budget does not have to mean foregoing comfort and elegance. Taiwan welcomes budget-conscious tourists with open arms, thanks to its varied choice of economical lodging alternatives. This book reveals budget-friendly pleasure all around the island, from comfortable hostels to budget-friendly guesthouses.

Hostels in the Lively Districts of Taipei

- Locations include Ximending, Zhongzheng District, and Da'an District

The dynamic areas of Taipei are peppered with budget-friendly hostels, which provide a great balance of cost and social environment. Among the highlights are:

- **Convenient Locations**: Hostels strategically positioned in major areas like Ximending, Zhongzheng, and Da'an allow you to stay in the thick of the activity.

- **Dormitory Design:** Choose dormitory-style lodging with shared amenities, which is ideal for single

66

© John D. Travelar

travellers or those looking for a communal experience.

- **Affordable Extras**: Many hostels provide complimentary facilities such as free Wi-Fi, social areas, and scheduled activities, which adds to the total value.

Cultural Enclave Guesthouses

- Departures from Jiufen, Tainan, and Lukang

Discover Taiwan's cultural hotspots while staying in budget-friendly guest houses that reflect local character. Among the features are:

- **Historical Ambiance:** Immerse yourself in the history of areas like Jiufen, Tainan, and Lukang, where guesthouses often reflect their surroundings' cultural legacy.

- **Local Perspectives**: Guesthouse hosts may be able to provide useful information on the finest local meals, hidden jewels, and cultural sites, boosting your trip experience.

- **Budget-Friendly Restaurants**: Discover budget-friendly cafes and street food stalls in these ethnic enclaves while tasting Taiwan's genuine tastes.

© John D. Travelar

Scenic Retreat Boutique Homestay**s**

- Sun Moon Lake, Alishan, and Kenting

Stay at boutique homestays set in lovely getaways to experience Taiwan's scenic splendour. Among the highlights are:

- **Proximity to Nature**: Wake up to breathtaking views of Sun Moon Lake, Alishan's woods, or Kenting's shoreline, giving a peaceful respite from the city.

- **Customised Service**: Boutique homestays often emphasise customised service, resulting in a pleasant and friendly environment for visitors.

- **Affordable Extravagances**: Enjoy inexpensive indulgences like warm rooms, garden areas, and local touches that will make your stay unforgettable.

Low-Cost Hotels in Major Cities

- Departures from Taichung, Kaohsiung, and Hualien

Taiwan's metropolitan centres include a variety of inexpensive hotels to meet the practical demands of budget-conscious guests. Among the features are:

- **Affordable Locations**: Budget hotels are often located in handy places, close to public transit, food choices, and urban attractions.

68

© John D. Travelar

- **Separate Rooms:** Choose from a choice of accommodation options, including private rooms with en-suite amenities that provide comfort and solitude at a low cost.

- **Local Explorations**: Use affordable motels as a base for exploring the different urban environments of Taichung, Kaohsiung, and Hualien.

Backpacker Inns on Scenic Trails

- Visit Taroko Gorge, Yushan National Park, and Yangmingshan

Stay at backpacker inns along Taiwan's picturesque trails for a low-cost excursion. Take a look at the following:

- **Trailside Lodging**: Backpacker inns are conveniently positioned along major routes, making them an excellent alternative for nature lovers and hikers.

- **Atmosphere of the Community**: Feel a feeling of community as you exchange tales and experiences with other travellers who share a love of outdoor adventure.

- **Affordable Packages**: Some backpacker inns provide budget-friendly packages that include guided treks, lunch, and lodging, making adventure planning easier.

© John D. Travelar

Taiwan's low-cost lodging alternatives allow visitors to experience the island's various landscapes, lively culture, and kind hospitality without breaking the bank. Affordable delight awaits every budget-conscious tourist, whether you're visiting metropolitan centres, cultural enclaves, or picturesque getaways.

FAQs

- 1. Are Taipei hostels ideal for families? While hostels are often geared at lone travellers and backpackers, some do provide family-friendly lodgings or private rooms suited for families. It is best to verify with the hostel ahead of time.

- 2. Can I locate low-cost hotels with English-speaking personnel in metropolitan areas like Kaohsiung? Yes, many low-cost hotels in major cities employ English-speaking personnel to help customers. Booking platforms and reviews may give information about the hotel staff's language proficiency.

- 3. Do boutique homestays in picturesque getaways provide transportation to guests? Some boutique homestays provide transportation or may help visitors in organising transportation to local attractions. When making reservations, it is best to ask about this.

- 4. Are there backpacker inns along picturesque routes that are suited for beginning hikers? Yes, several backpacker inns cater to inexperienced hikers by offering comfortable lodging and route information.

© John D. Travelar

When making a reservation, it is critical to explain your hiking experience and preferences.

- 5. Can I locate low-cost restaurants near guesthouses in ethnic enclaves? Yes, guesthouses in cultural enclaves are often placed near low-cost cafes and street food vendors, enabling tourists to sample local delicacies without breaking the bank.

© John D. Travelar

EXPLORING TAIPEI

Taipei, Taiwan's busy capital, is a city where history and modernity meet, producing a vibrant tapestry of experiences for visitors. This book is your passport to exploring Taipei's bustling streets and immersing yourself in the island's cultural lifeblood, from major monuments to hidden treasures.

Taipei 101- The Iconic Skyscraper and Beyond

- Address: Xinyi District

No trip to Taipei is complete until you see the architectural masterpiece that is Taipei 101. Among the highlights are:

- Observation Deck: Climb to the 89th level for magnificent views of the city and distant mountains.

© John D. Travelar

The vista is particularly beautiful at sunset and at night.

- Shopping Heaven: At the base, the Taipei 101 Mall is a premium shopping destination with foreign and Taiwanese brands. Enjoy a shopping frenzy or gastronomic treats at the mall's several eateries.

- Plaza Outside: The outdoor plaza is where activities and concerts take place. It's a terrific spot to unwind, take in the scenery, and participate in seasonal celebrations.

Chiang Kai-shek Memorial Hall- A Democracy Symbol

- Zhongzheng District is the location

Chiang Kai-shek Memorial Hall, dedicated to Taiwan's founding father, is both a symbol of democracy and a cultural icon. Key characteristics include:

- Changing of the Guard: Behold the stunning Changing of the Guard event, which takes place hourly in front of the main hall. Taiwanese military heritage is reflected in the accuracy and ceremonial.

- National Concert Hall and Theater: Investigate the nearby National Concert Hall and Theater, which hold cultural concerts and activities. These monuments' architectural splendour is worth appreciating.

© John D. Travelar

- Liberty Square: The area around Liberty Square is large and lushly green, giving a calm getaway in the centre of the city.

Ximending- Street Culture and Youthful Energy

- Location- Wanhua District

Ximending, sometimes known as the "Harajuku of Taipei," is a thriving area brimming with young energy and street culture. Explore:

- Extravaganza of Shopping: Explore the bustling streets lined with boutiques, fashionable stores, and street sellers. Ximending is a fashionista's and souvenir hunter's dream.

- Performances on the Street: Enjoy live music, street entertainment, and a dynamic environment. It is great for leisurely strolls due to the pedestrian-friendly streets.

- Cuisine Delights: At the various cafés and street food vendors, you may sample a wide range of local and foreign cuisines. Ximending is a foodie's paradise.

Beitou Hot Springs- A Natural Retreat

- Address: Beitou District

74

© John D. Travelar

Visit Beitou, which is famous for its geothermal hot springs, to get away from the rush and bustle of the city. Among the highlights are:

- Warm Spring Baths: Relax in one of the numerous hot spring resorts' public hot spring pools or rent a private bath. The mineral-rich waters have medicinal properties.

- Thermal Valley: Explore Thermal Valley, a natural hot spring region surrounded by beautiful foliage and boiling hot water. The unusual scenery is a photographer's dream.

- The Beitou Hot Springs Museum: The Beitou Hot Springs Museum, located in a magnificently preserved Japanese colonial building, tells the tale of Beitou's hot springs.

Longshan Temple- Wanhua's Spiritual Haven
- Location- Wanhua District

Longshan Temple, a famous and respected Buddhist temple in the centre of Wanhua District, is a spiritual retreat. Investigate its cultural significance:

- Architectural Wonders: Admire the temple's exquisite construction and artistic features, which represent a fusion of traditional Chinese and Taiwanese cultures.

© John D. Travelar

- Cultural Customs: Take note of the temple's cultural customs, such as prayer rituals and ceremonies. The temple is a site of worship as well as communal involvement.

- Concurrent Markets: To sample local street cuisine and vivid market life, visit the crowded marketplaces around Longshan Temple, such as Huaxi Night Market.

Elephant Mountain Hiking Trail- Panoramic Viewpoint of Taipei

- Address: Xinyi District

Elephant Mountain provides a pleasant hiking track with stunning vistas for nature lovers and photographers:

- Views of the Cityscape: Hike to the peak for breathtaking views of Taipei City and Taipei 101. The vista is especially beautiful during daybreak and sunset.

- Photography Possibilities: Capture Taipei's renowned skyline with the beautiful Taipei 101 as the focal point. The route offers several vantage points for stunning images.

- Nature and Fitness: The hiking path is easily accessible and suited for people of all fitness levels.

© John D. Travelar

It's a novel approach to connect with nature without leaving the city.

Taipei entices with a mix of cultural riches, contemporary wonders, and natural retreats. Taipei provides a broad assortment of activities for any tourist, whether you're exploring the heights of Taipei 101, immersing yourself in the spiritual milieu of Longshan Temple, or finding calm in Beitou's hot springs.

FAQs

- 1. Is it a good idea to buy Taipei 101 observation deck tickets in advance? Buying tickets in advance might help you avoid long lineups, particularly during peak hours. Purchasing tickets online or via hotel concierge services is often a handy alternative.

- 2. Does Ximending provide vegetarian eating options? Yes, Ximending has vegetarian and vegan eating alternatives. Many restaurants and street food booths cater to a variety of dietary needs.

- 3. Are tourists permitted to take part in the Changing of the Guard event at Chiang Kai-shek Memorial Hall? The Changing of the Guard event at Chiang Kai-shek Memorial Hall is open to the public. It's a free event in front of the main hall.

- 4. Are English-guided excursions of Beitou Hot Springs available? Yes, certain Beitou hot spring resorts provide English-guided excursions that

© John D. Travelar

provide information about the history and medicinal effects of the hot springs.

- 5. Is the Elephant Mountain Hiking Trail appropriate for beginners?Yes, the Elephant Mountain Hiking Trail is appropriate for novices, however it does have steps and steep portions. It is recommended that you wear comfortable shoes and carry water with you for the trek.

Must-Visit Landmarks

Taiwan, with its rich cultural past and different landscapes, has a tapestry of must-see attractions that enchant visitors. This book takes you on a trip to explore Taiwan's most famous and valued assets, from ancient temples to natural marvels.

Taroko Gorge is Nature's Grand Masterpiece.

- Hualien County is the location

Taroko Gorge, a natural wonder in eastern Taiwan, exemplifies the island's geological wonders. Investigate its magnificent features:

- Marble Canyons: Admire the Liwu River's steep cliffs and marble canyons sculpted over millions of years. Natural forms provide an enthralling scene.

© John D. Travelar

- The Shrine of Eternal Spring: Visit the Eternal Spring Shrine, set on a rock and dedicated to the remembrance of labourers who died while building the Central Cross-Island Highway.

- The Swallow Grotto Trail: Take a walk along the Swallow Grotto Trail, which is named for the rock formations that mimic swallow nests. The hike provides breathtaking views of the gorge.

Sun Moon Lake: Central Taiwan's Serenity

- Nantou County is the location

Sun Moon Lake, located in Taiwan's central highlands, is a tranquil and attractive resort. Among the highlights are:

- Cruise Knowledge: Take a boat ride on Sun Moon Lake to observe the surrounding mountains and the lake's merger of the sun and moon shapes.

- Ci'en Pagoda: Visit Ci'en Pagoda to get a bird's-eye perspective of the lake and its surroundings. The architecture of the pagoda echoes traditional Chinese aesthetics.

- Pier Shuishe: Explore the colourful Shuishe Pier district, which is noted for its lively ambiance, lakeside cafés, and local street cuisine.

© John D. Travelar

Jiufen Old Street: A Journey Through Time

- Place: New Taipei City

Jiufen Old Street is a lovely place that takes tourists back in time, set on a hillside overlooking the sea. Discover its one-of-a-kind offerings:

- Culture of the Teahouse: Walk through small alleys packed with traditional tea houses, souvenir stores, and street sellers to immerse yourself in teahouse culture.

- A-Mei Tea House: Visit the historic A-Mei Tea House, which has a rich history and breathtaking panoramic views. It was the basis for the animated feature "Spirited Away."

- Historical Atmosphere: Jiufen's architecture and cobblestone streets radiate historical beauty, providing a look into Taiwan's past.

National Palace Museum: An Art Treasure Trove

- Taipei City is the location

The National Palace Museum is a cultural jewel in Taipei, with a rich collection of Chinese art and antiques. Discover its wonders:

80

© **John D. Travelar**

- Imperial Jewels: Admire precious relics from numerous dynasties, such as ancient Chinese paintings, calligraphy, porcelain, and jade sculptures.

- Jadeite Cabbage: Behold the renowned Jadeite Cabbage, a little jade sculpture that has become an iconic emblem of the museum.

- Interactive exhibitions: Participate in interactive exhibitions that bring Chinese history and culture to life, offering a thorough grasp of the country's background.

Kenting National Park: Southern Tropical Paradise

- Pingtung County is the location

Kenting National Park, in southern Taiwan, is a tropical haven recognized for its breathtaking vistas and unique ecosystems. Discover its natural wonders:

- Lighthouse of Eluanbi: Visit the Eluanbi Lighthouse, Taiwan's southernmost point with magnificent views of the ocean. The region has a high level of ecological variety.

- Sheding Nature Park: Sheding Nature Park is well-known for its coral reefs, coastal woods, and hiking routes. The park is a paradise for birdwatchers and environment lovers.

© John D. Travelar

- Baisha Bay: Relax on the scenic beaches of Baisha Bay, which have turquoise seas ideal for swimming and water sports.

Longshan Temple is Taipei's spiritual oasis

- Address: Wanhua District, Taipei City

Longshan Temple is a famous and respected temple in Taipei that reflects traditional Taiwanese architecture. Learn about its cultural significance:

- An Architectural Wonder: Admire the temple's beautiful embellishments, which include a mix of Chinese and Taiwanese design elements.

- Religious Beliefs: Witness religious events and rituals, which provide insight into the local community's spiritual traditions.

- Cultural Festivals: Attend cultural festivals at Lungshan Temple, which include traditional performances, processions, and celebrations.

Taiwan's monuments create a tapestry of natural marvels, cultural riches, and historical treasures, beckoning visitors to discover the island's unique splendour. Whether you're admiring the marble canyons of Taroko Gorge, wandering through the nostalgic alleyways of Jiufen, or relaxing on the shores of Sun Moon Lake, each monument provides a distinct and rewarding experience.

© John D. Travelar

Culinary Delights in Taipei

Taipei, Taiwan's gastronomic capital, is a city where culinary traditions coexist with contemporary innovation. This book is your passport to explore Taipei's rich and delightful culinary environment, from crowded night markets to Michelin-starred restaurants.

Shilin Night Market: Night Market Delights

- Address: Shilin District

No gastronomic excursion in Taipei is complete without a stop at Shilin Night Market, a bustling foodie heaven. Explore the bustling street food scene:

- Oyster Omelets: Try the famous Taiwanese oyster omelette, a delectable blend of fresh oysters, eggs, and savoury sauce made perfectly on a scorching griddle.

- Smelly Tofu: Try stinky tofu, a fermented delicacy that, despite its unpleasant fragrance, provides a unique and flavorful sensation.

- Plenty of Bubble Tea: Enjoy a selection of bubble tea flavours and toppings, ranging from conventional milk tea to unique tastes and garnishes. Shilin Night Market is a hotspot for bubble tea fans.

© John D. Travelar

Din Tai Fung: Michelin-starred Dumplings

- Various locations, including Xinyi and Zhongshan districts

Din Tai Fung, a Taiwanese worldwide sensation, is famous for its delicious xiao long bao (soup dumplings). Immerse yourself in the world of Michelin-starred dumplings:

- Xiao Long Bao: Savour the delicate and juicy xiao long bao, each dumpling expertly constructed with a thin, translucent shell encasing a delicious soup and savoury contents.

- Broad Menu: Aside from dumplings, the menu includes truffle and pig dumplings, shrimp and pork shao mai, and exquisite noodle dishes.

- Experience with an Open Kitchen: Visit Din Tai Fung's open kitchen to see the craftsmanship that goes into preparing dumplings. The openness enhances the eating experience.

Raohe Street Night Market: A Culinary Adventure

- Address: Songshan District

Raohe Street Night Market is a gastronomic wonderland that offers a diverse selection of Taiwanese street cuisine. Set off on a culinary adventure:

© John D. Travelar

- Black Pepper Buns: Queue for black pepper buns, a delicious treat made with seasoned pork enclosed in a crisp pastry shell and freshly cooked in cylinder ovens.

- Squid Grilled: Grilled squid on a stick is a popular street food dish that is seasoned with a combination of spices, giving the shellfish a smokey and savoury depth.

- Ice Cream Rolls with Mochi: Mochi, a chewy rice cake, and ice cream rolls, in which a small layer of ice cream is beautifully folded within a delicate crepe, are also available.

Aquatic Development Addiction: Seafood Extravaganza

- Address: Zhongshan District

Addiction Aquatic Development is a gourmet paradise for seafood lovers, delivering a one-of-a-kind seafood market and dining experience:

- Market for Seafood: Explore the bustling fish market, which has a selection of fresh seafood. Select your favourites and have them cooked to your specifications.

© John D. Travelar

- Sushi Bar: The sushi bar offers a premium sushi experience with the freshest cuts of sashimi and sushi masterfully created by trained chefs.

- Oyster Bar: Succulent oysters are served in the oyster bar, along with a range of condiments and sauces. The oysters' freshness attests to Taiwan's coastal richness.

Modern Tea Houses: A Combination of Tradition and Innovation

- Various locations, including Songshan and Da'an Districts

Modern tea shops in Taipei provide a modern spin to traditional tea culture. Experience a seamless fusion of innovation and tradition:

- High Mountain Oolong: Enjoy the flowery tones and delicate taste of high mountain oolong tea. Premium teas are often sourced from Taiwan's hilly areas by modern tea shops.

- Tea Pairing Menus: Explore tea matching meals that enrich the tea-drinking experience by combining teas with delightful nibbles or sweets.

- Demonstrations of Tea Brewing: Attend tea brewing demos to learn about the art of tea preparation, from

© **John D. Travelar**

selecting the perfect leaves to mastering the pour-over.

The culinary scene in Taipei is a symphony of tastes, textures, and scents that highlight the island's rich food culture. Taipei delivers a gourmet voyage unlike any other, whether you're relishing the legendary xiao long bao at Din Tai Fung, going on a street food adventure at Raohe Street Night Market, or indulging in the finest seafood at Addiction Aquatic Development.

Shopping Hotspots

Taipei, a lively city, is a shopping haven for people of all tastes and styles. This guide reveals the main shopping areas that characterise Taipei's retail scene, from busy street markets to upmarket malls.

Ximending

- Location- Wanhua District

Ximending, sometimes known as the "Harajuku of Taipei," is a stylish area that caters to both the fashionable and the culturally inclined:

- Fashion Stores: Discover a multitude of fashion stores showcasing the newest trends, one-of-a-kind streetwear, and eccentric designs. Ximending is a sanctuary for urban stylish fashionistas.

© John D. Travelar

- Performances and Street Art: Immerse yourself in the bustling street art culture and live acts that contribute to the dynamic mood of the neighbourhood. Ximending is a cultural hotspot where fashion and art collide.

- Local Brands and Independent Stores: Discover Taiwanese companies and independent stores that highlight Taipei's design scene's originality and ingenuity. It's a great place to find one-of-a-kind products.

Taipei 101 Mall

- Address: Xinyi District

Taipei 101 Mall, located at the foot of the landmark Taipei 101 tower, is a premium shopping destination for discriminating shoppers:

- Fashion Houses Around the World: Shop for luxury from worldwide fashion companies such as Chanel, Louis Vuitton, and Gucci. The Taipei 101 Mall is a display of high-end elegance.

- Designer Shops: Explore designer stores that provide a carefully chosen collection of apparel, accessories, and lifestyle items. For those looking for exquisite and special things, the mall is a haven.

© John D. Travelar

- Fine Dining: Gourmet eating is available at the mall's upmarket restaurants, which provide a variety of world cuisines. The gastronomic experience fits the opulent retail environment.

Shilin Night Market

- Address: Shilin District

Shilin Night Market is not just a gastronomic paradise, but also a lively market full with discounts and one-of-a-kind local treasures:

- Stalls for Fashion and Accessories: Stroll around the market's lively lanes, which are lined with vendors selling low-cost apparel, accessories, and unusual products. Bargaining is a frequent practice in this country.

- Local Craftspeople: Discover local craftsmen' handcrafted products and beautiful masterpieces. Shilin Night Market is a great opportunity to support local artisans and acquire unique gifts.

- Shopping and Street Food: Combine your shopping experience with a gourmet trip. Many kiosks provide various types of street food, enabling you to refuel while exploring the market.

Wufenpu Garment Wholesale Area

- Address: Songshan District

© John D. Travelar

Wufenpu Garment Wholesale Area is a lively neighbourhood noted for its wholesale and retail garment market for individuals looking for low-cost fashion:

- Wholesale Cost: Enjoy wholesale discounts on a variety of apparel products ranging from casual wear to formal outfits. It's a haven for bargain hunters and people trying to update their wardrobe on the cheap.

- Trendy Looks: Explore the current fashion trends at Wufenpu, where you'll find a variety of designs to suit all preferences. To remain abreast of fashion trends, the district is continually developing.

- Footwear and Accessories: Wufenpu also sells accessories, footwear, and fashion needs in addition to apparel. It's a one-stop shop for a whole fashion makeover.

Guang Hua Digital Plaza

- Zhongzheng District is the location

Guang Hua Digital Plaza is a must-see site for tech aficionados and gadget fans, showcasing the newest in electronics and technology:

- Electronics Stores: Explore many floors of electronics stores that sell a broad selection of items such as

© John D. Travelar

computers, cellphones, gaming equipment, and accessories. The plaza is a tech haven.

- Services for Customization: Some stores in Guang Hua provide customisation services, such as building your own PC or personalizing your electronics. It's a paradise for tech-savvy folks looking for one-of-a-kind solutions.

- Gaming and Virtual Reality Experiences: Immerse yourself in different stores' gaming and virtual reality experiences. Guang Hua is a vibrant environment where you may try and explore the newest in technological innovation.

Taipei's retail districts appeal to a wide range of tastes, from luxury shoppers to bargain hunters and tech aficionados. Taipei provides a shopping trip unlike any other.

© John D. Travelar

BEYOND TAIPEI

While Taipei is a thriving cultural and innovation centre, exploring outside the city reveals Taiwan's hidden beauties and cultural treasures. This book welcomes you to experience the various splendor that lies outside Taipei's city boundaries, from natural beauties to historic landmarks.

Sun Moon Lake

- Nantou County is the location

Sun Moon Lake, located in Taiwan's central highlands, is a calm refuge surrounded by beautiful scenery. Discover the tranquil beauty and cultural richness:

- Boat Tours: Take a leisurely boat ride on Sun Moon Lake, where the sun and moon's combining forms provide breathtaking vistas. The boat journey is a relaxing experience that allows you to take in the natural splendor.

- Ci'en Pagoda: Ci'en Pagoda, a historic monument with panoramic views of the lake and its surroundings, is worth a visit. The building of the pagoda embodies traditional Chinese aesthetics and offers a tranquil place for introspection.

- Pier Shuishe: Wander around Shuishe Pier, the lake's primary core, where you'll discover lakeside cafés, souvenir stores, and a lively atmosphere. It's an excellent location to learn about local culture.

Jiufen

- Place: New Taipei City

Jiufen is a lovely village built on a mountain overlooking the sea that takes tourists back in time. Discover its nostalgic streets and cultural highlights:

- Culture of the Teahouse: Walk through tiny alleys dotted with historic tea houses, souvenir stores, and street sellers to immerse yourself in the teahouse culture. Jiufen's tea houses have a rich history.

- A-Mei Tea House: Visit the famous A-Mei Tea House, which offers panoramic views of the coastline and historical value. The teahouse was inspired by the animated film "Spirited Away."

© John D. Travelar

- Evenings with Lanterns: Experience Jiufen's lovely environment in the evening, when lanterns illuminate the small alleyways, creating a romantic and nostalgic aura.

Kenting National Park

- Pingtung County is the location

Kenting National Park, located in southern Taiwan, is a tropical paradise recognized for its breathtaking scenery and various ecosystems. Immerse yourself in nature's splendor:

- Lighthouse of Eluanbi: Explore the Eluanbi Lighthouse at Taiwan's southernmost tip. The lighthouse provides breathtaking views of the sea and the rough shoreline.

- Sheding Nature Park: Discover Sheding Nature Park, a nature lover's paradise with coral reefs, coastal woods, and hiking paths. The park is a haven for birdwatchers and outdoor enthusiasts.

- Baisha Bay: Relax on the sandy beaches of Baisha Bay, which is noted for its clean beaches and blue seas. It's an excellent location for swimming, snorkeling, and other water sports.

A patchwork of natural beauty, cultural riches, and historic places await exploration outside Taipei's urban pulse. Whether

© John D. Travelar

cruising on Sun Moon Lake, marvelling at the marble canyons of Taroko Gorge, experiencing Jiufen's nostalgic charm, basking in the tropical beauty of Kenting National Park, or delving into Tainan's historical richness, Taiwan's hidden gems offer a journey of discovery and wonder.

Cultural Gems in Taichung

Taichung, located in the centre of Taiwan, is a city that perfectly mixes history and contemporary, providing adventurous travellers with a treasure trove of cultural pearls. This book allows you to discover the rich cultural tapestry that makes Taichung a distinctive destination, from medieval temples to modern art galleries.

The National Taichung Theater

- Address: Xitun District

The National Taichung Theater was constructed by famous architect Toyo Ito and serves as a beacon of contemporary art and innovation:

- Futuristic Style: Admire the theatre's contemporary and organic form, which resembles a huge cloud or bubble. The fluidity and curves of the structure provide a visual spectacle both inside and out.

© John D. Travelar

- Venue for Performing Arts: Investigate the inside, which features cutting-edge facilities for numerous performing arts. From classical concerts to contemporary dance, the theatre showcases a variety of programs.

- Open Areas: Take use of the public areas around the theatre, such as the outdoor plaza and water features. These sites serve as meeting places for cultural activities.

Rainbow Village

- Address: Nantun District

Huang Yung-Fu, a whimsical artist, has converted Rainbow community, which was formerly a military dependents' community, into a vivid living art installation:

- Vibrant Murals: Stroll through the small streets lined with vivid paintings of animals, figures, and creative situations. Each painting offers a different narrative and contributes to the attractiveness of the community.

- Artistic Preservation: Take part in a grassroots initiative to conserve culture via the medium of art. Rainbow Village is an example of how creativity may be used to preserve history and community spirit.

© John D. Travelar

- Photography Haven: Take Instagram-worthy pictures against a background of vibrant colours and creative emotions. Rainbow Village is a popular destination for photographers and art lovers alike.

Lin Family Mansion and Garden

- North District Location

The Lin Family Mansion and Garden, built during the Qing Dynasty, is a well-preserved historic landmark that showcases traditional Taiwanese architecture and landscaping:

- Architectural Glamour: Explore the beautifully built houses, courtyards, and halls that mirror the Qing Dynasty architectural style of affluent Taiwanese households.

- Organic Gardens: Explore the spacious grounds, which include pavilions, ponds, and lush foliage. Traditional landscaping techniques help to create a peaceful and harmonious atmosphere.

- Exhibitions of Culture: Visit the on-site museum, which has cultural items and exhibitions about the Lin family and the Qing Dynasty. Gain insight into Taiwan's cultural heritage.

Taichung Confucius Temple

- Central District Location

© John D. Travelar

The Taichung Confucius Temple is a cultural and educational centre devoted to the legendary philosopher Confucius.

- Architectural Magnificence: Admire the beautiful carvings, elegant roofing, and traditional courtyards of ancient Chinese architecture. The temple's design is evocative of old Chinese Confucius temples.

- Cultural Ceremonies: Attend cultural ceremonies and activities in the temple that promote Confucianism's ideals. These gatherings often feature traditional music, dancing, and ceremonies.

- Programs for Education: Explore the temple's educational offerings, which range from calligraphy instruction to cultural seminars. The temple serves as a cultural and artistic hub for Chinese people.

Miyahara
- Central District Location

Miyahara, once a Japanese colonial-era ophthalmology clinic, has been turned into a cultural and gastronomic destination:

- Architecture Inspired by Europe: Admire Miyahara's architectural elegance, which combines Japanese and European design elements. The red-brick structure is a lovely combination of history and modernity.

- Ice Cream Confections: Indulge in scrumptious ice cream at the on-site ice cream shop, where the flavors and presentation are a visual and sensory feast. Miyahara's ice cream is a gourmet delight not to be missed.

- Tea Culture and Retail: Discover Miyahara's many stores and tea-related merchandise. The restaurant is not only a gastronomic joy, but it is also a place to learn about tea culture and tradition.

From the historic grandeur of the Lin Family Mansion to the modern elegance of the National Taichung Theater, Taichung's cultural pearls provide a mesmerising trip through time. Taichung encourages you to experience its unique cultural environment, whether you're immersed in the living art of Rainbow Village, enjoying the cultural richness of the Confucius Temple, or tasting ice cream pleasures at Miyahara.

Natural Wonders in Hualien

Hualien, located on Taiwan's gorgeous east coast, is a paradise for nature lovers and adventure seekers. The area is rich in natural treasures, ranging from stunning coastline scenery to lush national parks. Join us on a tour through the amazing natural wonders of Hualien, where each turn reveals a new dimension of Taiwan's beautiful splendor.

© John D. Travelar

Taroko Gorge

- Place: Taroko National Park

Taroko Gorge, a natural marvel inside Taroko National Park, exemplifies the island's geological wealth and visual grandeur:

- Marble Canyons: Admire the gorge's magnificent marble rocks, formed by the Liwu River over millions of years. The canyons' sheer size produces a stunning sight.

- The Swallow Grotto Trail: Set off on the Swallow Grotto Trail, a trail that goes through the valley and provides stunning views of the blue river and towering rock formations. Keep an eye out for the cliff-nesting swallows.

- The Shrine of Eternal Spring: Visit the Eternal Spring Shrine, built on a cliffside and dedicated to labourers who died while building the Central Cross-Island Highway. The placement of the shrine affords panoramic views of the surrounding environment.

Qingshui Cliffs

- Xiulin Township is the location

The Qingshui Cliffs, located along Highway 11, exhibit the rocky nature of Taiwan's eastern coast:

© John D. Travelar

- Extreme Cliff Faces: Consider the steep vertical cliffs that fall spectacularly into the deep blue Pacific Ocean. The cliffs, which reach heights of almost 800 meters, are breathtaking.

- Natural Coastal Drive: Take a picturesque drive down Highway 11, which hugs the shore and provides breathtaking views of the Qingshui Cliffs. The trip is a visual feast of natural beauty in and of itself.

- Cingshuei Zih Shoreline Park: Visit Cingshuei Zih Shoreline Park for a closer look at the cliffs and a chance to photograph the stunning surroundings. The park offers a peaceful backdrop for admiration and photography.

Taroko National Park

- Location: Taroko National Park, Various Trails

Taroko National Park is home to the famed Taroko Gorge as well as a network of charming paths that lead to hidden gems:

- Shakadang Pathway: Hike the Shakadang Trail, which is known for its clear river and tall marble cliffs. The route reveals the area's geological beauties as well as insights into the local culture.

- Waterfall Trail in Baiyang: Explore the Baiyang Waterfall Trail, which leads to a beautiful waterfall tucked in a lush forest. The trek is made more

101

© John D. Travelar

exciting by the inclusion of tunnels and suspension bridges.

- Old Jhuilu Trail: The Jhuilu Old Trail is a tough hike with beautiful views of the canyon for the more courageous. The walk traverses small ledges and provides an unusual view of Taroko's landscapes.

Liyu Lake

- Address: Shoufeng Township

Liyu Lake, a picturesque reservoir surrounded by mountains and trees, provides a pleasant respite from the city:

- Scenic Peace: Enjoy the peace and quiet of Liyu Lake, where the calm waters mirror the lush surroundings. The lake is great for a leisurely walk, picnics, and photographing the scenery.

- Bicycle trail: Ride your bike around the lake, following the specific trail that encircles the reservoir. The bike ride offers magnificent vistas and an opportunity to interact with nature.

- Birdwatching Possibilities: Birdwatchers will enjoy the variety of bird species that inhabit the lake's ecology. The tranquil ambiance makes it an ideal site for bird watching and photography.

Stone Mountains

- Yuli Township is the location

© John D. Travelar

Sixty Stone Mountain, called for its distinctive rock formations, exemplifies Taiwan's geological diversity:

- Limestone Pillars That Have Eroded: Admire the mountain's worn limestone pillars, which resemble ancient totems. Geological formations reveal the natural processes that created the area over millennia.

- Trails for Hiking: Hiking routes weave around the mountain, enabling tourists to get up close and personal with the unusual rock formations. The paths range in difficulty, catering to varied hiking inclinations.

- Views from Above: Climb to the peak of the mountain for panoramic views of the surrounding valleys and mountains. The viewpoint offers a spectacular view of Hualien's natural splendor.

Hualien's natural beauties, from the dramatic gorges of Taroko Gorge to the coastal grandeur of Qingshui Cliffs, the calm refuge of Liyu Lake, the geological marvels of Sixty Stone Mountain, and the captivating trails of Taroko National Park, present a vivid picture of Taiwan's various landscapes. Hualien welcomes you to go on a voyage of discovery.

Historical Sites in Tainan

© John D. Travelar

Tainan, Taiwan's oldest city, is a living reminder of the island's rich history and cultural legacy. This city is steeped in history and welcomes tourists to wander through time, discovering ancient temples, historical sites, and architectural marvels. Join us on a tour through Tainan's historical tapestry, where every turn reveals a new chapter in the city's illustrious history.

Chihkan Tower

- Address: West Central District

Chihkan Tower, also known as Fort Provintia, is a historic landmark that witnesses the city's complicated history under numerous colonial powers:

- Dutch Inflection: Explore the ruins of Dutch colonial buildings from the 17th century, when the Dutch East India Company erected Fort Provintia. The tower acted as an administrative hub.

- Chinese rebuilding: See the Qing Dynasty's Chinese-style rebuilding of Chihkan Tower, which was used as a government office. The mix of architectural styles reflects the city's varied history.

- Exhibitions of Historical Interest: Visit the on-site museum, which displays historical relics, cultural exhibitions, and information about the city's position as a cultural and economic centre throughout history.

104

Anping Old Fort

- Address: Anping District

The Anping Old Fort, also known as Fort Zeelandia, is a well-known fortification that played an important part in Taiwan's nautical history:

- Dutch Period Relics: Explore the ruins of the Dutch East India Company's Fort Zeelandia, which formerly existed on the site. During the Dutch colonial era, the stronghold served as a strategic outpost.

- Historical Structures: Walk around the centuries-old walls of Anping Old Fort, which have seen a lot of alteration. The well-preserved buildings provide insight into military architecture from many times.

- Fortification Grounds: Stroll around the fort's expansive grounds, which include historical plaques, cannons, and calm gardens. The location affords magnificent views of the surrounding region.

Koxinga Shrine

- Address: West Central District

The Koxinga Shrine, dedicated to Ming Dynasty hero Zheng Chenggong (Koxinga), is a revered and historical site:

- Ming Dynasty Relationship: Learn about Zheng Chenggong's life and accomplishments as he fought

© John D. Travelar

against the Qing Dynasty and built the Kingdom of Tungning. His contributions to Taiwan's history are commemorated at the shrine.

- Architectural Glamour: Admire the shrine's classic Chinese architectural characteristics, such as elaborate carvings, elegant roofing, and tranquil courtyards. The design is in the style of the Ming Dynasty.

- Cultural Ceremonies: Attend cultural ceremonies and activities hosted at the shrine, particularly around significant historical anniversaries. The location serves as a focal point for commemorating Taiwan's Ming Dynasty past.

National Taiwan Literature Museum

- Address: West Central District

The National Museum of Taiwan Literature is a cultural institution dedicated to Taiwan's literary accomplishments and linguistic diversity:

- Historic Structure: Explore the museum's historic edifice, which was previously the Office of the Governor-General during the Japanese colonial period. The architecture is a fusion of Japanese and Western elements.

- Exhibits of Literature: Explore exhibitions featuring the works of Taiwanese writers, poets, and literary

© John D. Travelar

luminaries. The museum honors the island's rich literary tradition in a variety of languages.

- Interactive Displays: Immerse yourself in interactive displays and multimedia installations that bring books to life. For visitors of all ages, the museum provides a lively and engaging experience.

Kuantu Folk Arts Center

- Address: Anping District

The Kuantu Folk Arts Center is a cultural centre devoted to the preservation and promotion of traditional Taiwanese folk arts:

- Classical Performances: Traditional performances, such as puppet shows, folk music, and theatrical plays, should be attended. The centre's mission is to rehabilitate and promote Taiwanese traditional arts.

- Interactive Workshops: Participate in hands-on workshops to learn traditional crafts including puppetry, paper cutting, and traditional musical instruments. The centre promotes active participation in cultural heritage.

- Cultural Exchange: Participate in the centre's cultural exchange activities, which create links between local communities and tourists interested in Taiwan's traditional arts.

© John D. Travelar

Tainan's ancient landmarks constitute an enthralling patchwork that demonstrates the city's tenacity and cultural continuity despite centuries of change. Tainan's historical tapestry invites exploration and appreciation, from the Dutch influences at Chihkan Tower to the maritime legacy of Anping Old Fort, the Ming Dynasty reverence at Koxinga Shrine, the literary celebration at the National Museum of Taiwan Literature, and the folk arts revival at Kuantu Folk Arts Center.

© John D. Travelar

OUTDOOR ADVENTURES

Taiwan is a paradise of outdoor delights for adventure seekers and environment aficionados, with a diversified terrain that appeals to a variety of adrenaline levels. The island invites visitors seeking adrenaline-pumping adventures and immersive natural experiences, with towering peaks and flowing waterfalls. Join us as we explore the outdoor experiences that Taiwan's gorgeous environment has to offer.

Hiking Trails and National Parks

Taiwan's natural splendor unfolds via a network of hiking routes inside its national parks, providing an outdoor enthusiast's paradise. Each route, from towering peaks to tranquil lakes, offers a tale about the island's different environments. Join us for a hike through Taiwan's national

© John D. Travelar

parks, where every step reveals beautiful panoramas and a connection with nature.

Yangmingshan National Park

- Area: Northern Taipei

Yangmingshan National Park is famed for its volcanic scenery, hot springs, and brilliant flower displays, and is situated close north of Taipei:

- Qixing Mountain Trail: Climb Qixing Mountain, Yangmingshan's highest peak, via the Qixing Mountain Trail. Hikers are rewarded with spectacular views of the surrounding mountains and the Taipei basin on the trek.

- The Lengshuikeng Trail: Discover the Lengshuikeng Trail, which is famous for its unusual volcanic landscape and fumaroles. As you travel through heated vents and boiling mud pots, you will have an unearthly experience.

- Blooming Season: During the flower season (spring and early summer), the park's slopes are festooned with blossoming azaleas, cherry blossoms, and other bright flowers.

Shei-Pa National Park

- Area: Central Taiwan

© John D. Travelar

The centre mountain range's Shei-Pa National Park is a sanctuary for visitors seeking alpine scenery and undisturbed wilderness:

- Xue Mountain (Snow Mountain): Set out on the Xue Mountain Trail, which will take you to the major peak, East Xue. The difficult walk provides breathtaking alpine landscapes, high mountain meadows, and the exhilaration of reaching one of Taiwan's highest peaks.
- Dabajian Mountain: Take a hike to Dabajian Mountain, which is recognized for its unusual rocky summit. The path winds through lush woods, across rivers, and culminates in an exciting climb to the top, which offers stunning views of the surrounding peaks.

- Extension Trails Taroko Gorge: Explore the Taroko Gorge extension paths, such as the Baiyang Trail and the Swallow Grotto Trail. These routes have a variety of sceneries, such as waterfalls, marble cliffs, and lush flora.

Yushan National Park
- Area: Central Taiwan

Yushan National Park is home to Taiwan's tallest peaks, difficult treks, and breathtaking views:

- Main Peak Trail: The Main Peak Trail leads to Yushan (Jade Mountain), Taiwan's highest peak. The hike

© John D. Travelar

includes high-altitude trekking, alpine meadows, and a feeling of achievement at the top.

- East Peak of Mt. Jade: Consider trekking to Mt. Jade East Peak for a less crowded but equally gratifying experience. The hike provides breathtaking views of Yushan's main peak and neighbouring mountains.

- Holly Ridge Trail: The Holy Ridge Trail is a multi-day hike that covers the high-altitude ridges of Yushan. The walk offers breathtaking vistas and an opportunity to explore the park's different ecosystems.

Kenting National Park

- Area: Southern Taiwan

Kenting National Park, situated on Taiwan's southernmost point, provides coastal paths, coral reefs, and a tropical getaway:

- Trail of the Eluanbi Lighthouse: Explore the Eluanbi Lighthouse Trail, which runs down Taiwan's rough coastline to the island's southernmost tip. The route offers breathtaking views of the ocean, rocks, and the famous lighthouse.

- Shedding Nature Park: Hike through Shedding Nature Park, which has coastal paths that lead to sandy beaches, unusual rock formations, and coral reefs.

The park combines natural beauty with cultural history.

- Coastal Trail in Longpan Park: The Longpan Park Coastal Trail provides a scenic stroll along the cliffs overlooking the Pacific Ocean. The route is well-known for its wildflowers and stunning views of the vast coastline.

Taroko National Park

- Area: Eastern Taiwan

Taroko National Park is a natural paradise with marble canyons, towering cliffs, and a complex route network:

- Zhuilu Ancient Trail: Hike the Zhuilu Old Trail, which clings to the cliffs above Taroko Gorge for an exciting trip. The hike offers breathtaking views of the gorge and its marble cliffs.

- Waterfall Trail in Baiyang: Explore the Baiyang Waterfall Trail, which leads to a beautiful waterfall tucked among lush flora. The path has tunnels, suspension bridges, and opportunities to explore the park's different ecosystems.

- Trail Lushui-Heliu: Immerse yourself in the Lushui-Heliu Trail, which follows the Liwu River and provides breathtaking views of marble formations, waterfalls, and the Taroko Gorge's spectacular sceneries.

© John D. Travelar

Taiwan's national parks are a treasure trove of hiking paths, each with its own distinct combination of natural beauties and adventure. These routes offer hikers to experience the many landscapes that characterise the island's beautiful outdoors, from the alpine heights of Yushan to the seaside beauty of Kenting, and the marble wonders of Taroko to the volcanic landscapes of Yangmingshan.

Water Activities and Beaches

Taiwan's diversified coastline, highlighted by golden beaches and blue seas, entices sun-soaked adventurers. The island provides a variety of coastal enjoyment, from exhilarating water sports to calm beach getaways. Join us as we discover the aquatic sports and picturesque beaches that make Taiwan a sea lover's paradise.

Kenting National Park

- Area: Southern Taiwan

Kenting National Park, with its tropical temperature and diverse marine life, is a water sports paradise:

- Jialeshui Windsurfing: At Jialeshui, a popular windsurfing area, feel the wind in your hair and ride the waves. It is great for both beginners and expert

© John D. Travelar

windsurfers because of the constant winds and pristine seas.

- Longpan Park Snorkeling: Dive into Longpan Park's crystal-clear waters for a snorkeling excursion. Explore Taiwan's southern coast's gorgeous coral reefs, unique marine life, and undersea treasures.

- Coastal Trail of Maobitou: Hiking the Maobitou Coastal Trail combines coastal exploration with aquatic sports. Cliff diving chances are available on the path, providing an exciting element to the gorgeous coastal environment.

Fulong Beach

- Area: Northeastern Taiwan

Fulong Beach is a popular location for surfers and beachgoers due to its golden beaches and regular waves:

- Surfing Instruction: Fulong Beach offers surfing training so you can ride the waves. The beach's consistent surf conditions make it an ideal location for novices to practise this thrilling water activity.

- The Gold Coast Bikeway: Discover the Golden shore Bikeway, a gorgeous riding path that goes along the shore. The bike path gives stunning views of the water and quick access to Fulong Beach and its neighbouring attractions.

115

© John D. Travelar

- Fulong Sand Sculpture Art Festival: Every year, artists build elaborate sculptures from the beach's golden sands, bringing a cultural flavour to the seaside experience.

Baishawan Beach

- Area: Northern Taiwan

Baishawan Beach, with its immaculate white beaches and bustling environment, is a popular beach and sports destination:

- Beach Volleyball: Play beach volleyball on one of Baishawan's well-kept courts. The large width of the beach allows for both competitive and leisure play.

- Kayaking at Sea: At Baishawan, sea kayaking allows you to explore the coastal waterways. Paddle around the beach, admiring the sights of the water and the surrounding countryside.

- Active Atmosphere: Experience Baishawan's dynamic environment, particularly on weekends when residents and visitors alike congregate to enjoy the sun, sea, and different seaside activities.

Jibei Island

- Location: Off Keelung's Coast

Jibei Island is a quiet island hideaway with beautiful seas and magnificent coral reefs:

© John D. Travelar

- Scuba Diving and Snorkelling: Snorkeling or diving will allow you to experience the underwater splendor of Jibei Island. The clean waters display a kaleidoscope of coral formations and marine life, making for an unforgettable aquatic adventure.

- Camping on the Beach: Camping on the beach allows you to enjoy the calm of the island. On Jibei Island, beachfront camping is a popular pastime that allows guests to stargaze and wake up to the sound of calm waves.

- Cultural Discovery: Discover the cultural highlights of the island, such as historic temples and local fish markets. Jibei Island provides a look into the relaxed way of life of a distant coastal hamlet.

Dawulun Beach

- Area: Northeastern Taiwan

Dawulun Beach, located in the Northeast Coast Scenic Area, is a tranquil haven with breathtaking sunset views:

- Relaxation on the Beach: Relax on the tranquil sands of Dawulun Beach, away from the hustle and bustle of the city. The calm environment of the beach makes it perfect for leisurely strolls and moments of relaxation.

© John D. Travelar

- Picnics at Sunset: Pack a picnic and watch the sunset from the beach. The vivid colours of the setting sun, mixed with the sound of lapping waves, make a romantic or family-friendly atmosphere for an evening.

- Cycling on the Beach: Cycle along the established bike routes to discover the coastal splendor of the Northeast Coast Scenic Area. Dawulun Beach is a great place to start for picturesque rides with panoramic ocean views.

From the windswept beaches of Kenting to the surfing utopia of Fulong, the isolated sanctuary of Jibei Island, and the tranquil beauty of Dawulun Beach, Taiwan's coastal pleasures provide a diverse range of water sports and beach retreats. Taiwan's coasts are ideal for seaside pleasure, whether you're looking for action in the surf or a peaceful escape by the water.

Cycling Routes

Taiwan's varied surroundings, from towering mountains to sweeping sea views, make it a cyclist's dream. The island's network of well-maintained bike paths provides scenic splendor as well as varied terrain for cyclists of all abilities. Join us as we cycle around some of Taiwan's most beautiful roads, where each pedal stroke reveals a new aspect of the island's natural treasures.

© John D. Travelar

Sun Moon Lake Cycling Trail

- Nantou County is the location

The Sun Moon Lake Cycling Trail around the gorgeous Sun Moon Lake, offering bikers the ideal combination of lakefront peace and highland beauty:

- Smooth Routes: Enjoy a nice riding journey around the lake on well-paved routes. The route is simple to follow and suited for cyclists of all skill levels.

- Lakefront Views: Take in the breathtaking scenery of Sun Moon Lake's beautiful waters surrounded by lush mountains. The shifting environment, from lakeside temples to deep woodlands, provides a magical touch to the journey.

- From Shuishe Pier to Ita Thao Village: Begin your tour from Shuishe Pier and cycle to Ita Thao Village. Stop at gorgeous places like Ci'en Pagoda for panoramic views and Xuanguang Temple for cultural discovery along the route.

East Rift Valley Bikeway

- Area: Eastern Taiwan

The East Rift Valley Bikeway winds across the scenic East Rift Valley, taking bikers through coastal grandeur and pastoral landscapes:

© John D. Travelar

- Coastal Views: Start off by riding down the coast, with the Pacific Ocean on one side and the Coastal Mountain Range on the other. The spectacular ocean vistas provide a picturesque background for the first portion of the journey.

- Rural Charm: Ride through picturesque rural settings, past enormous rice paddies, pineapple plantations, and tiny towns. The route encapsulates Taiwan's landscape, delivering a pleasant and immersive riding experience.

- Section Fuli to Yuli: Discover the Fuli to Yuli area, which is noted for its beautiful landscape and cultural attractions. Continue through the valley's gorgeous scenery after visiting the Fuli Market, famous for its handcrafted traditional umbrellas.

Taroko Gorge Cycling Path

- Area: Eastern Taiwan

The Taroko Gorge Cycling Path immerses riders in Taroko National Park's awe-inspiring magnificence, presenting towering marble cliffs and lush mountain landscapes:

- Marble Wonders: Ride through Taroko Gorge's core, where marble cliffs rise abruptly on each side of the road. The gorge's enormous grandeur and fascinating marble formations combine to offer a spectacular riding experience.

© John D. Travelar

- The Swallow Grotto Trail: Discover the Swallow Grotto Trail, a brief yet stunning portion of the bicycle trail. Admire the marble-walled canyon and the Liwu River below, with stops to take in the spectacular view.

- Nine Turns Tunnel: The Tunnel of Nine Turns, a meandering portion of the route that takes riders through a succession of tunnels built into the slope, is a challenge. Each bend provides a different view of the gorge.

Pingxi Crags Cycling Route

- Area: Northern Taiwan

The Pingxi Crags Cycling Route reveals northern Taiwan's raw grandeur, including coastline cliffs, underground caverns, and cultural gems:

- Coastal Area of Jinshan: Begin your adventure at the Jinshan Coastal Area, where the path follows the cliffs overlooking the Pacific Ocean. A relaxing cycling experience is provided by the fresh sea wind and breathtaking ocean vistas.

- Undiscovered Caves and Temples: Along the way, look for secret caves and temples to give a cultural flavour to your cycling journey. Shitoushan Park is a

121

© John D. Travelar

great place to explore the unusual rock formations and take in the views of the shoreline.

- Fisherman's Wharf: Finish your trip to Danshui's Fisherman's Wharf, a busy waterfront district noted for its seafood and boisterous ambiance. Relax along the water's edge and think of the coastal beauty you've seen on your trip.

Kenting National Park

- Area: Southern Taiwan

Kenting National Park provides a bicycle path that mixes coastal delights with tropical vistas, creating a one-of-a-kind mixture of natural beauty:

- Eluanbi writes to Maobitou: Begin your journey at Eluanbi, Taiwan's southernmost tip, then cycle your way to Maobitou. The path hugs the coastline, providing breathtaking views of the craggy cliffs, crystal-clear seas, and lush flora.

- Coastal Trail in Longpan Park: Longpan Park Coastal Trail is a bicycle path that travels through coastal grasslands and provides panoramic views of the Pacific Ocean. The path is especially beautiful at daybreak and sunset.

- Kenting Night Market: Finish your bicycle excursion at the bustling Kenting Night Market. Celebrate the

122

© **John D. Travelar**

end of your seaside excursion by indulging in local cuisine and taking in the colorful environment.

Taiwan's cycling routes cater to a wide range of tastes, from the tranquillity of Sun Moon Lake to the awe-inspiring grandeur of Taroko Gorge, the offshore attractiveness of the East Rift Valley to the hidden treasures along the Pingxi Crags Cycling Route, and the tropical surroundings of Kenting National Park. Each route offers a unique cycling experience, revealing the picturesque delights of the island one pedal at a time.

© John D. Travelar

TAIWANESE CUISINE

Taiwanese cuisine is a harmonic fusion of tastes, textures, and culinary traditions reflecting the island's numerous cultural influences. Taiwan provides a gourmet adventure that tantalises taste senses and celebrates the essence of indigenous delicacies, from street-side booths to sophisticated restaurants. Join us as we begin on a gastronomic journey through the rich tapestry of Taiwanese food.

Night Market Delights

Taiwan's colorful night markets are a gastronomic heaven, with indigenous specialties taking centre stage among busy vendors and boisterous ambiance:

- Smelly Tofu: To enjoy stinky tofu, a Taiwanese delicacy, brave the unpleasant fragrance. Deep-fried to perfection, it has a crispy outside and a soft inside, and it is often served with pickled cabbage and a drizzle of sauce.

- Oyster Omelet: Oyster omelettes, a popular street food option, are savoury delights. A tasty and pleasant meal is created by combining plump oysters, eggs, and a starchy sauce.

- Sparkling Tea: Bubble tea, Taiwan's renowned product, will quench your thirst. For a refreshing and sweet beverage, choose from a selection of tea bases, add chewy tapioca pearls, and modify sweetness levels.

Beef Noodle Soup

Beef noodle soup, considered a national dish, has a specific position in Taiwanese cuisine:

- Perfect Broth: The broth is the core of beef noodle soup, cooked to perfection with a combination of spices, soy sauce, and soft bits of beef. The richness of taste and perfume is a monument to culinary skill.

- Noodle Styles: Enjoy the craftsmanship of noodle-making with beef noodle soup's diversity of noodle varieties, which range from thin and chewy to thick and substantial. Each variant adds a distinct flavour to the hearty broth.

© John D. Travelar

- Additional Information: Accompaniments such as pickled mustard greens, cilantro, and chile oil may be used to enhance your gastronomic experience. These offer layers of texture and contrast to the soup's rich tastes.

Xiao Long Bao

Soup dumplings, or Xiao Long Bao, are a delicate and savoury culinary creation:

- Thin Skins and Juicy Fillings: The thin, delicate skins of Xiao Long Bao encase a blast of delicious soup and luscious beef filling. The dumplings are meticulously prepared to attain the ideal texture and flavour balance.

- Harmony of Dipping Sauces: Dip Xiao Long Bao in a combination of soy sauce, vinegar, and ginger to enhance the flavour. The dipping sauce both compliments and adds acidity to the flavorful soup.

- A Wide Range of Fillings: While pork is the classic filling, Xiao Long Bao also comes in crab, shrimp, and vegetarian flavours. Each variety adds a distinct flavour to this dumpling delicacy.

Lu Rou Fan (Braised Pork Rice)

Lu Rou Fan, or braised pork rice, is a hearty and savoury Taiwanese dish:

126

© John D. Travelar

- Perfect Braised Pork: The braised pork is savoury and soft, cooked in a rich sauce of soy sauce, garlic, and spices. Slow cooking ensures that the meat absorbs the rich marinade, resulting in a delectable meal.

- Flavour Balance: As the braised pork is served over a bed of steamed rice, enjoy the balance of flavours. The sweetness of the sauce, paired with the savoury pork, results in a delightful and soothing gastronomic experience.

- Optional Additions: To add depth and texture to this simple but substantial meal, customise your Lu Rou Fan with extra toppings such as a tea-boiled egg or pickled veggies.

Street Food Delights

The busy streets of Taiwan come alive with a symphony of sizzling woks, tantalising fragrances, and the joyous conversation of residents and tourists alike. Taiwanese street food is more than just a fast snack; it's a culinary adventure, a celebration of tastes that tantalise taste senses and highlight the island's gourmet ingenuity. Join us as we stroll through the lively streets, savouring the enticing pleasures of Taiwanese street cuisine.

© John D. Travelar

Crispy and Flavorful Scallion Pancakes

Scallion pancakes are a popular street dish, with a crispy surface and layers of delicious goodness:

- Flaky Layers: The layers of the pancake are magical, formed by rolling and folding the dough with scallions and oil. This produces a flaky, but chewy texture that is really gratifying.

- Dipping Sauces: Scallion pancakes go well with dipping sauces like soy sauce, vinegar, or chilli-infused oil. The combination of the savoury pancake with the tangy or spicy flavours of the sauce results in a delectable gastronomic experience.

- A Wide Range of Fillings: Some sellers take scallion pancakes to the next level by adding fillings like shredded radish or minced pork, which enhances the taste profile and adds tactile contrast.

Oyster Vermicelli

Oyster vermicelli, also known as o-a-mi-sua, is a delightful noodle soup that celebrates Taiwan's love of seafood:

- Briny Delight: The fresh oysters are unquestionably the centrepiece of this meal, giving a salty and succulent layer to the mild and starchy broth. The vermicelli noodles provide a delicate foundation for the rich flavours.

© John D. Travelar

- Topping: Peanut PowderMany sellers add peanut powder over oyster vermicelli, providing a nutty and somewhat sweet contrast to the salty soup. It's a distinguishing feature that enhances the food.

- Accompanying Condiments: Dress up your bowl with condiments like garlic, vinegar, and chile to customise the taste. Adding these condiments interactively increases the whole experience.

Gua Bao

Gua Bao, often known as the Taiwanese burger, is a tasty and portable treat that embodies Taiwanese street food:

- Steamed Soft Buns: Gua Bao is made out of pillowy steamed buns that cradle a delectable blend of ingredients. The softness of the buns complements the flavorful contents well.

- Pork Belly Braised: The basic filler for Gua Bao is braised pig belly, which melts in your tongue. Pickled mustard greens, ground peanuts, and cilantro are often used to create a perfect combination of tastes and textures.

- Enjoyment on the Street: One of the pleasures of Gua Bao is its mobility, which allows you to appreciate its delectableness while wandering through congested streets or standing at a noisy night market. It's a classic street food experience.

Taiwanese Sausages

Taiwanese sausages, or xiangcheng, are a popular street snack with a smokey taste and a variety of spice options:

- Perfectly Grilled: The sausages are usually grilled, which gives them a smoky, somewhat sweet taste. The grilling method imparts a delightful snap with each mouthful, making them popular among both residents and visitors.

- Flavor Variety: Taiwanese sausages come in a variety of tastes, including the traditional original as well as ones flavoured with garlic, herbs, or even wasabi. Each version has a distinct flavour that appeals to a wide variety of palates.

- Additional Information: Taiwanese sausages go well with garlic, fresh herbs, or a touch of soy sauce. These modest additions improve the whole experience, enabling you to fully appreciate the tastes.

Stinky Tofu

Stinky tofu, also known as chou doufu, is a fragrant and strong street snack that is not for the faint of heart:

- Goodness Fermented: The fermenting process, which produces a unique and pungent scent, gives stinky

© John D. Travelar

tofu its name. The tofu is perfectly deep-fried, resulting in a crunchy surface that contrasts with the soft and creamy centre.

- Additional Information: Pickled cabbage, soy sauce, and occasionally chilli are common accompaniments to stinky tofu, enabling you to modify the taste profile. The spicy tofu combined with the acidic pickled cabbage provides a distinct and distinctive flavour.

- Culinary Expedition: Trying stinky tofu is a gastronomic adventure, and although the smells may take some getting used to, many people find the pungent tastes to be a satisfying and genuine Taiwanese street food experience.

Taiwan's street food culture is a lively tapestry of tastes, ranging from crispy layers of scallion pancakes to the saline richness of oyster vermicelli, the portable ecstasy of Gua Bao, the grilled perfection of Taiwanese sausages, and the daring gastronomic adventure of stinky tofu. Each mouthful is a tribute to the island's culinary prowess, asking you to join the symphony of street food pleasures.

Regional Specialties

Taiwan's culinary environment is a dynamic mosaic of tastes, with each area providing distinctive delicacies that highlight the island's numerous cultural influences. Exploring Taiwan's

© John D. Travelar

regional specialties is a gourmet tour that reveals the rich tapestry of local ingredients and culinary traditions, from the busy streets of Taipei to the tranquil coastline villages. Join us on a fascinating trip as we sample the various flavours of each locale.

Taipei: Gourmet Mecca of Street Delights

- Main Dish: Beef Noodle Soup

The bustling metropolis of Taipei is a gastronomic wonderland where traditional tastes and new culinary trends collide:

- Beef Noodle Soup: Taipei is famous for its delicious and fragrant beef noodle soup. The rich broth, tender meat, and properly cooked noodles create a taste symphony that exemplifies the city's culinary brilliance. Spicy beef noodle soup and clear broth alternatives are available to suit diverse taste preferences.

- Xiao Long Bao: The world-famous Din Tai Fung restaurant chain started in Taipei. A characteristic meal that has received worldwide praise is Xiao Long Bao, exquisite soup dumplings packed with delicious broth and minced pork.

- Delights of the Shilin Night Market: Explore the lively Shilin Night Market for a plethora of street cuisine treats ranging from oyster omelettes to sizzling star-shaped chicken nibbles. Taipei is a street

© John D. Travelar

food nirvana because of the variety of snacks and small nibbles available.

Tainan: Taiwanese Cuisine's Cradle

- Danzai Noodles are the signature dish.

Tainan, regarded as the birthplace of Taiwanese cuisine, is rich in culinary traditions and historical influences:

- Danzai Noodles: Danzai noodles, Tainan's trademark cuisine, is a substantial bowl of noodles topped with minced pork, shrimp, and a delicious broth. The dish was inspired by the city's historical importance as a Qing Dynasty capital.

- Coffin Bread: Coffin Bread is a distinctive Tainan dish in which a large slab of bread is hollowed out, stuffed with delicious ingredients like fish or curry, then deep-fried to golden perfection.

- Taiwanese Milkfish: Freshwater milkfish is a local delicacy that is often grilled, stewed, or served in a soup. Tainan's closeness to the sea means that high-quality seafood is readily available.

Hualien: Land and Sea Abundance

- Mochi Rice Cuisine is the restaurant's signature dish.

133

© John D. Travelar

Hualien, located between the Central Mountain Range and the Pacific Ocean, provides a gastronomic experience that honors both land and marine bounty:

- Mochi Rice Cuisine: Hualien is famous for its Mochi Rice Cuisine, which consists of sticky rice formed into different shapes and served with a variety of toppings. This one-of-a-kind eating experience demonstrates the diversity of rice in Taiwanese cuisine.

- Fresh Seafood from the Ocean: Hualien has a variety of fresh seafood meals due to its proximity to the shore. Seafood aficionados may taste the flavours of the Pacific Ocean with anything from grilled squid to sushi.

- Ancient Influences: The cuisine of Hualien is also inspired by its indigenous inhabitants. Indigenous products and culinary skills give the local food scene a particular flavour.

Chiayi: A Chicken Rice Lovers' Paradise

- Chiayi Chicken Rice is the restaurant's signature dish

Chiayi, in southern Taiwan's lush plains, is a sanctuary for chicken rice fans:

- Chiayi Chicken Rice: The city is famous for its tender and tasty chicken rice. The chicken is cooked

134

© John D. Travelar

to perfection and served with aromatic rice, as well as a side of minced garlic, soy sauce, and, for an extra kick, chilli sauce.

- Turkey Rice: Another local favourite is Turkey Rice, which consists of delicate chunks of turkey served over a bed of rice. Chiayi's agricultural wealth is reflected in the meal, as is the usage of locally bred fowl.

- Porridge with Frog Legs: Chiayi serves frog leg porridge to the adventurous diner, highlighting the city's numerous gastronomic choices. The frog legs are tenderly cooked and served in a delicious porridge.

Yunlin: Vegetarian Culinary Paradise

- Specialty Dish: Vegetarian Delights

Yunlin, noted for its agricultural and variety products, provides a one-of-a-kind dining experience with a vegetarian focus:

- Vegetarian Specialties: Yunlin is a vegetarian food lover's delight. The area embraces the tastes of fresh vegetables and plant-based components, from vegetarian hot pot to meatless renditions of classic cuisine.

© John D. Travelar

- Yunlin is well-known for its soy sauce, which is used in a variety of local foods. Slow-cooked tofu, mushrooms, and other ingredients are simmered in a savoury soy sauce broth to create meals that are both delectable and nutritious.

- Snacks and Fruits: Fruits and snacks are also abundant in the region's agricultural riches. Visitors may taste locally produced fruits and a variety of vegetarian snacks that emphasise Yunlin's devotion to plant-based nutrition.

Taiwan's regional specialties demonstrate the island's culinary variety, reflecting each region's own history, topography, and cultural influences. Each area provides a gastronomic adventure that captivates the senses, from the gourmet joys of Taipei to the historical tastes of Tainan, the richness of Hualien, the chicken rice refuge of Chiayi, and the vegetarian delights of Yunlin.

Dining Etiquette

Taiwanese eating etiquette is a difficult balancing act that reflects the island's unique cultural tapestry and focus on harmony. Understanding and honouring local eating traditions improves the whole gourmet experience, whether you're in a crowded night market or an expensive restaurant. Join us as we learn the intricacies of eating etiquette in Taiwan, where every meal is a cultural event.

© John D. Travelar

Seating Arrangements

Seating patterns communicate respect and status in Taiwanese society. Important factors to remember:

- First and foremost, the Elders: Elders have traditionally been accorded precedence, and it is typical for them to be seated first. If you are a visitor, you should wait for instructions on where to sit.

- Outward Facing: The most prestigious seat is one that faces the entryway or a gorgeous view. It is often designated for distinguished visitors or the head of the household.

- Personal Space: When seated, keep a comfortable distance from others. Personal space is highly valued in Taiwanese society, therefore avoiding invading someone else's territory.

Handling of Chopsticks

Chopsticks are an essential item in Taiwanese eating, and knowing how to handle them correctly is critical:

- There will be no pointing: Both pointing your chopsticks at people and leaving them sticking up in a dish of rice are deemed disrespectful.

- Food Passing: When sharing meals, it's usual to pick up and move food to someone else's plate using the opposite end of your chopsticks.

© John D. Travelar

- Do Not Play with Chopsticks: Resist the impulse to tap your chopsticks on the table or play with them, since these activities are considered rude.

Table Manners

Consideration for those at the table is valued in Taiwanese eating etiquette:

- Await Elders: Begin eating just after the elders or host have begun. This shows appreciation for their contribution to the dinner.

- Dishes to Share: Taiwanese dinners are often communal, with dishes placed in the middle of the table for sharing. When accepting meals, use serving utensils or the other end of your chopsticks.

- Quiet Enjoyment: Maintain a reasonable volume in talks, particularly in more formal situations. It is considered nice to eat quietly with no noisy distractions.

Tea Culture

Tea is an important component of Taiwanese dining, and knowing tea etiquette improves the whole experience:

- Providing Tea: It is usual for the younger or lower-ranking person at the table to give tea to the elderly or higher-ranking folks.

138

© John D. Travelar

- Tea Acceptance: When someone gives you tea, softly tap the table with your fingers in thanks. This is a customary manner of thanking someone.

- Tea Pouring: When serving tea to others, begin by serving those who are older or of greater social rank. As a demonstration of respect, hold the teapot with both hands.

Declining Politeness

If you're served a food you don't want to eat, politely refusing is an art:

- Express Your Appreciation: Express your appreciation for the offer politely. You have the option of saying "thank you" or "I appreciate it."

- There's No Need for Extensive Excuses: It is not required to provide comprehensive reasons for denying a food. In most cases, a simple and kind refusal is adequate.

- Focus on Other meals: Draw attention to other meals you appreciate or express a desire to explore a new specialty.

Taiwanese eating etiquette is a graceful, respectful, and considerate dance. Embracing these customs enriches not only your food experience but also helps you to immerse yourself in Taiwan's cultural diversity. Let the rhythm of Taiwanese

© John D. Travelar

dining etiquette lead you through a delicious culinary adventure, whether you're sampling street cuisine in a noisy night market or enjoying a formal dinner.

© John D. Travelar

CULTURAL EXPERIENCES

Taiwan, a compelling East Asian island, offers a rich tapestry of cultural experiences that entice visitors to discover its customs, festivals, and creative manifestations. Taiwan takes you on a voyage of cultural immersion, from flamboyant festivals that light up the streets to peaceful temples steeped in history. Let us unwrap the one-of-a-kind cultural experiences that await those eager to explore the heart and spirit of this enthralling island.

Temple Festivals
Taiwan's temples are not just places of prayer, but also dynamic cultural hubs:

- Pilgrimages to Mazu: Witness the splendor of Mazu pilgrimages, in which followers march in procession in honour of the sea goddess Mazu. A compelling

© John D. Travelar

spectacle is created by elaborate parades, martial arts demonstrations, and traditional music.

- Halloween Festivals: Lantern celebrations, which take place throughout the Lunar New Year, light up the night sky. Lanterns with intricately carved wishes engraved on them are launched, producing a beautiful show of colour and light.

- Ghost Month Events: Temples hold festivities to pacify wandering ghosts during Ghost Month. Traditional performances, opera performances, and the burning of phantom money are all part of these celebrations.

Indigenous Cultural Villages
Taiwan's indigenous peoples have kept their distinct customs alive, and visiting cultural villages gives you a glimpse into their way of life:

- Tribe of Atayal: Wulai Village of the Atayal Tribe is famed for its hot springs and traditional architecture. Participate in traditional dance performances and learn how to make complex handwoven fabrics.

- Tribe of the Paiwan: Visit the Paiwan Tribe in Pingtung, which is known for its vivid festivals and unique wood sculptures. Traditional Paiwan rites and the Laiyi Green Tunnel give an authentic cultural experience.

© **John D. Travelar**

- Amis Folk Center: At the Amis Folk Center in Hualien, you may immerse yourself in Amis culture. Participate in traditional artisan classes, sample indigenous food, and learn about the tribe's traditions and ceremonies.

Traditional Tea Culture
Taiwanese tea culture is a tranquil journey that blends tea making with periods of reflection:

- Jiufen Tea Houses: Jiufen, an ancient village with tiny alleyways, is home to traditional tea shops with seaside views. While surrounded by ancient charm, savour oolong tea.

- Plantations of Pinglin Tea: Explore Pinglin's tea estates, which are famed for producing high-quality oolong tea. Take part in tea tastings, learn about tea manufacturing, and relax in the beautiful green sceneries.

- Tie Guan Yin Muzha Tea: Visit Muzha, which is well-known for its Tie Guan Yin tea. Experience a traditional tea ceremony, in which the preparation and presentation of tea becomes an art form, encouraging attention and connection.

National Palace Museum
The National Palace Museum in Taipei is a cultural jewel, with a rich collection of Chinese art and artefacts:

© John D. Travelar

- Early Chinese Artefacts: Over 700,000 ancient Chinese treasures, including paintings, calligraphy, pottery, and jade, are on display. The collection in the museum covers 8,000 years of Chinese history.

- Jadeite Cabbage: Behold classic works such as the Jadeite Cabbage, a masterfully carved jadeite sculpture representing wealth and fertility. Each detail demonstrates the Qing Dynasty's workmanship.

- Changing Exhibits: The museum has changing exhibits, giving a fresh experience with each visit. The shows demonstrate the range of Chinese cultural heritage, ranging from rare texts to royal garments.

Traditional Markets

Traditional markets in Taiwan are vibrant places where cultural experiences develop amid the hustle and bustle:

- Shilin Night Market: Immerse yourself in the bright mayhem that is Shilin Night Market in Taipei. Taste local street cuisine ranging from stinky tofu to oyster omelettes while watching street entertainers contribute to the colorful ambiance.

- Jinguashi Gold Ecological Park: Jinguashi, a historic gold mining village, is worth a visit. Explore the Gold Museum, the Crown Prince Chalet, and the historic alleys that reflect the island's mining history.

© John D. Travelar

- Dihua Street Market: Immerse yourself in the ancient beauty of Taipei's Dihua Street Market. The market, which is known for its traditional stores selling dry products, herbs, and textiles, provides a look into Taiwan's commercial history.

Taiwan's cultural experiences invite you to enter a world where traditions are respected, celebrations illuminate the night, and creative expressions transcend time. Taiwan invites you to immerse yourself in its rich cultural tapestry, temple festival, enjoying tea in a calm environment, seeing indigenous cultural villages, marvelling at old relics, or navigating the lively pandemonium of traditional markets.

Traditional Festivals

During its traditional holidays, Taiwan comes alive with a kaleidoscope of colours and customs. These vibrant festivals are steeped in history, mythology, and religious customs, providing a window into the heart and soul of the island's different populations. Join us on an exploration of Taiwan's traditional festivals, where each event is a colorful thread in the fabric of the island's cultural identity.

Lunar New Year

The Spring Festival, also known as Lunar New Year, commemorates the beginning of the lunar calendar and is Taiwan's most important traditional festival:

© John D. Travelar

- Family Gatherings: Families assemble for elaborate feasts, and red envelopes (hongbao) are exchanged for good luck. Traditional delicacies like Chinese dumplings and gao (rice cake) add to the joyful mood.

- Lion and Dragon Dances: Dragon and lion dances fill the streets, thought to fend off bad spirits. As colorful parades weave through villages, the rhythmic rhythms of drums and cymbals fill the air.

- Lanterns and Fireworks: Fireworks light up the night sky, signifying the removal of darkness. Lantern festivals, which include artistically constructed lanterns, contribute to the visual extravaganza.

Ghost Month

The Hungry Ghost Festival, also known as Ghost Month, is a month-long celebration devoted to honouring ancestors and soothing wandering spirits:

- Ghost Stories: Ghost operas are elaborate performances conducted in open settings. Traditional Chinese operas are said to amuse and appease spirits.

- Rituals and Offerings: Families give food, incense, and symbolic gifts to their ancestors. Floating lanterns and water lantern releases are typical activities used to lead souls back to the afterlife.

© John D. Travelar

- Prohibitions and Precautions: To avoid meetings with wandering spirits, traditional taboos such as not swimming or staying out late are enforced. The ghost realm is said to be closer to the living during Ghost Month.

Lantern Festival

The Lantern Festival, also known as the Yuanxiao Festival, concludes the Lunar New Year festivities with a spectacular display of lanterns:

- Detailed Lantern Displays: Cities and villages are decked with elaborate lantern displays of all forms and sizes. Traditional themes, zodiac symbols, and new patterns pique the interest of the viewer.

- Lanterns in the Sky: The launch of sky lanterns is a highlight, particularly in Pingxi. Visitors write their wishes on lanterns before releasing them into the night sky, producing a captivating scene as the lanterns drift into the night sky.

- City Parades: The celebratory mood is enhanced by vibrant street parades including traditional music, dancing, and cultural displays. The Lantern Festival is a visually stunning celebration of light and togetherness.

147

© John D. Travelar

Dragon Boat Festival

The Dragon Boat Festival, also known as the Duanwu Festival, mixes exciting dragon boat racing with traditional rites such as:

- Dragon Boat Competitions: Long, thin boats ornamented with dragon heads are paddled aggressively by teams. The races, which take place in Taiwan's rivers and lakes, represent the quest for the renowned poet Qu Yuan.

- Zongzi: Zongzi, pyramid-shaped rice dumplings covered in bamboo leaves, are a traditional celebration meal. These are often packed with either sweet or savoury ingredients.

- Poetic Beginnings: The event honors poet Qu Yuan, who died in the Miluo River. People hurried to rescue him, giving rise to the custom of dragon boat races and tossing rice dumplings into the water to keep fish from devouring his corpse.

Mazu Pilgrimages

Mazu Pilgrimages are magnificent processions devoted to the sea goddess Mazu, a venerated divinity who is said to protect fishermen and sailors:

- Extensive Processions: Devotees go on pilgrimages, carrying the Mazu statue in elaborate processions that

© John D. Travelar

may span hundreds of kilometres. Traditional music and performances add to the joyful ambiance.

- Spiritual Importance: Pilgrimages often include rituals to obtain blessings for safe passage at sea and a plentiful harvest. The voyage is both a religious and cultural event that draws both participants and observers.

- Achievement at Temples: The pilgrimages conclude at Mazu temples, where rites, prayers, and celebrations take place. It is a time when communities gather together to commemorate and thank the sea goddess.

Traditional holidays in Taiwan are an enthralling combination of old traditions, vivid performances, and social festivities. Each holiday adds to the cultural tapestry that distinguishes Taiwan, from the grandeur of Lunar New Year to the light of Lantern holiday, the respect of Ghost Month, the excitement of Dragon Boat Festival, and the spiritual importance of Mazu Pilgrimages. Accept the festivities, see the customs, and join in the vivid celebrations that weave the fabric of Taiwan's cultural history.

Temples and Religious Practices

Taiwan's cultural fabric is a complicated tapestry of religious beliefs and rituals. The religious environment of the island is as varied as its inhabitants, with grandiose temples situated

© John D. Travelar

amid busy towns and peaceful mountain chapels. Join us on a tour across Taiwan's temples and religious customs, where old traditions combine effortlessly with contemporary life, resulting in a spiritual balance that is peaceful.

Temple Architecture

Taiwan's temples are architectural wonders that showcase excellent workmanship and detailed decoration, reflecting a combination of numerous influences:

- Classic Rooflines: Temples often have unique roof lines that are ornamented with ornate carvings and bright embellishments. The tiered roofs and upward-curving eaves are both symbolic and visually beautiful.

- Phoenix and Dragon Motifs: Dragon and phoenix themes are common, representing strength and elegance. These mythological animals are often beautifully carved onto temple pillars, door frames, and facades.

- Altars and Statues: Temples have altars devoted to different deities, as well as statues of gods and goddesses. The sculptures are meticulously constructed, and the materials used, such as wood, stone, or metal, vary.

150

Worship and Rituals

Taiwanese religious traditions include a variety of rites and ceremonies that are practised with dedication and reverence:

- Offerings of Incense: Incense burning is a widespread practice that represents cleansing and communion with the divine. Incense sticks are placed in enormous urns by devotees, generating aromatic clouds that float around temple grounds.

- Blessings and Chants: Worshippers give prayers and chants in order to get blessings, seek direction, or show appreciation. The repetitive sound of prayers and the melodic resonance of chants help to create a peaceful ambiance inside temples.

- Celebrations of the Lunar New Year: During the Lunar New Year, temples are especially alive, with unique rituals done to usher in the new year. These celebratory days are marked by fireworks, entertainment, and processions.

Feng Shui and Temple Location

Feng Shui concepts are important in deciding temple placement and layout, resulting in a harmonious interaction between the building and its surroundings:

- Water and Mountains: Many temples are carefully located near mountains and bodies of water, with the notion that these natural components provide

© John D. Travelar

beneficial energy. Mountains provide protection, whilst water represents riches and success.

- Nature Alignment: Temples are often associated with geographical elements, such as facing a certain direction or being located along ley lines. This alignment is said to boost the flow of positive energy, or qi.

- impact on Design: Feng Shui principles impact not just the placement of temples but also their design. The layout of hallways, courtyards, and entrances is meticulously designed in order to maximise energy flow and create a feeling of harmony.

Festivals and Processions

Taiwan's religious calendar is peppered with vivid festivals and processions that unite communities in celebration:

- Festivals of Tianhou (Mazu): The most extravagant processions are those devoted to the sea deity Mazu. Devotees parade the statue of the god through the streets, followed by music, dancing, and ceremonial acts.

- The Zhongyuan Festival: This event, also known as Ghost Month, includes rites and processions to commemorate ancestors and wandering souls.

Traditional performances, such as ghost operas, provide the observances a cultural component.

- Birthday Parties: Temples hold extravagant celebrations to commemorate the birthdays of deities. Elaborate processions decked with ornate floats weave their way through streets, attracting throngs of both residents and visitors.

Pilgrimages

Pilgrimages are important in Taiwanese religious activities, with devotees travelling to seek blessings and demonstrate devotion:

- Pilgrimage to Dajia Mazu: The Dajia Mazu Pilgrimage, one of the most renowned pilgrimages, spans a path of over 300 kilometres. Thousands of people join the parade, which is famous for its intensity and the transport of a large palanquin.

- Pilgrimage to Xiaolin Village: The spiritual value of the Xiaolin Village Pilgrimage leads participants through stunning landscapes and old paths. Pilgrims set off on their trip with a spirit of piety and brotherhood.

- Pilgrimage to Jiufen Wangye: The Jiufen Wangye Pilgrimage honors the soil deity Wangye. Pilgrims walk through Jiufen's ancient centre, praying for

© John D. Travelar

protection and prosperity. The journey incorporates spirituality and cultural discovery.

Temples and religious traditions in Taiwan are an important component of the island's cultural character, offering a look into the spirituality that pervades everyday life. Temples in Taiwan are not merely places of worship; they are living expressions of tradition and peace, whether they are ornamented with exquisite carvings, pulsating with rhythmic chanting, or holding vivid festivals.

Arts and Performances

Taiwan is a refuge for arts and performances that represent its unique cultural past. Taiwan's cultural environment is a kaleidoscope of inventiveness, ranging from traditional Chinese opera to modern art displays. Join us on a trip through the arts and performances on the island, where old traditions collide with cutting-edge expressions to create a vibrant and compelling cultural environment.

Traditional Chinese Opera

Traditional Chinese opera has strong roots in Taiwanese culture, combining music, theatre, and visual arts in a compelling blend:

- The Peking Opera: Peking Opera is a famous art form in Taiwan, known for its lavish costumes, painted faces, and acrobatic dances. Performances often

154

© John D. Travelar

reflect historical or mythical tales, highlighting a diverse cultural tapestry.

- Taiwanese Opera: Taiwanese opera, which has its roots in local folk customs, incorporates bright costumes and artistic makeup. The melodious songs and various singing techniques distinguish it as a distinct and beloved cultural manifestation.

- The Hakka Opera: Hakka Opera, notable for its colorful performances and usage of the Hakka language, is a contribution to Taiwan's opera scene by the Hakka ethnic minority. These operas often deal with love, loyalty, and historical events.

Contemporary Art Exhibitions

Taiwan's contemporary art scene is a vibrant mash-up of creativity, experimentation, and cultural entanglement:

- The Taiwan Fine Arts Museum: The Taipei Fine Arts Museum, as a contemporary art centre, organises a variety of exhibits showcasing local and international artists. The museum's dedication to displaying cutting-edge works adds to Taipei's international reputation as a cultural hotspot.

- Songshan Cultural and Creative Park The Songshan Cultural and Creative Park, housed in a former tobacco factory, is a dynamic area that holds art exhibits, design events, and cultural festivals. The

© John D. Travelar

park exemplifies Taiwan's dedication to encouraging innovation and creative expression.

- Biennial Celebrations: Taiwan's involvement in international art biennials such as the Taipei Biennial and the Asian Art Biennial gives artists a platform to participate in global discourses. These events draw artists, curators, and art lovers from all over the globe.

Puppetry and Shadow Theater

Puppetry and shadow theatre are old techniques of storytelling that continue to attract audiences:

- Budaixi Glove Puppetry: Glove puppetry is a traditional art form that mixes music, conversation, and skilled puppet handling with finely constructed puppets. The stories are often based on historical legends and folktales.

- Piyingxi Shadow Theater: Casting shadows on a screen to create dynamic and visually appealing storytelling is what shadow theatre is all about. The utilisation of complex cut-out characters and light manipulation adds to the story's richness.

- Contemporary Interpretations: Taiwanese puppeteers are recreating ancient traditions by integrating them with new themes and methods. Puppetry will remain a vital and relevant art form as a result of its dynamic progression.

156

© John D. Travelar

Traditional Dance and Martial Arts

Traditional dance and martial arts in Taiwan are more than just physical exercises; they are manifestations of cultural heritage:

- Chinese Classical Dance: traditional Chinese dance, which is based on traditional Chinese aesthetics, is distinguished by flowing movements, expressive gestures, and sophisticated footwork. Traditional myths and legends are often used as inspiration for performances.

- Taiji (Tai Chi): Tai Chi, an ancient Chinese martial art, is also practised as a mindful movement and meditation technique. People practising Tai Chi fill parks around Taiwan, generating a feeling of camaraderie and well-being.

- Folk Dancing: Taiwan's many ethnic groups contribute to the island's unique tapestry of folk dances. These dances are often performed in conjunction with celebrations, festivals, and rituals, and they serve as a visual representation of cultural variety.

Music Festivals

Taiwan's music scene is a genre melting pot, and music events highlight the island's musical diversity:

© John D. Travelar

- Music Center of Taiwan: The Taipei Music Center is a live performance venue that hosts concerts, recitals, and music festivals. The centre offers a platform for a broad spectrum of musical expressions, from classical symphonies to modern pop.

- Summer Wave Music and Art Festival: The Spring Wave Music and Art Festival is an annual celebration of Taiwanese and Asian pop music. The event draws music fans with its broad array of performers and bands.

- Golden Independent Music Awards: The Golden Indie Music Awards promote innovation and originality in the music business by recognizing and rewarding independent performers. The awards event serves as a showcase for both rising and veteran performers.

© John D. Travelar

SAFETY AND HEALTH TIPS

As you go out to discover Taiwan's natural beauty and cultural riches, your safety and well-being are of the utmost importance. Taiwan is a safe place to visit. However, being knowledgeable and prepared is essential for a pleasant and enjoyable journey. Let's look at some important safety and health precautions to assist you traverse Taiwan with confidence.

Emergency Information

While Taiwan is a safe and inviting location, unexpected events might occur while travelling. Being prepared and knowledgeable about emergency protocols is critical for a safe and enjoyable vacation. Let's look at important emergency information for Taiwan visitors to ensure you're prepared for any unforeseen emergencies.

© John D. Travelar

Emergency Phone Numbers

- Police Department: Dial 110 to contact the police in the event of a criminal occurrence, an accident, or an imminent danger to your safety. The operators may provide English assistance and arrange appropriate replies.

- Fire and EMS: Dial 119 in the event of a medical emergency, a fire, or the need for an ambulance. To assist a timely response, provide detailed information about the incident, your location, and any particular specifics.

- Tourist Information Line: 0800-011-765 the Tourist Hotline is a service targeted to travellers that provides support in a variety of languages, including English. This hotline may be used for general queries, reporting missing things, or learning about local services.

Medical Assistance

- Hospitals and Clinics: Taiwan has an advanced healthcare system that includes sophisticated hospitals and clinics. Consider going to a reputed hospital or clinic if you want medical assistance. Because many medical personnel in Taiwan know English, communication is easier.

- Pharmacies: In Taiwan, pharmacies are extensively accessible. Pharmacists may help with minor illnesses

© John D. Travelar

and sell over-the-counter drugs. If you have prescription drugs, keep them in their original packaging and have a list of generic names handy.

- Medical Evacuation in an Emergency: Medical evacuation services may be requested in extreme medical crises. It is critical to have comprehensive travel insurance that includes medical evacuation coverage to ensure you obtain quick and specialist treatment if necessary.

Natural catastrophes

- Typhoons: Typhoons strike Taiwan, particularly during the typhoon season, which lasts from June to October. Keep up with weather predictions, obey any cautions or evacuation orders, and have an emergency kit ready with items such as water, nonperishable food, and first aid supplies.

- Earthquakes: Taiwan is positioned in an earthquake-prone area. Learn about earthquake safety precautions such as "Drop, Cover, and Hold On." Locate secure areas in buildings and pay attention to any official statements or alarms.

General Safety Recommendations

Safety on the Road: Taiwan's traffic is well-regulated, however it is essential to respect traffic regulations whether walking or riding. To maintain road safety, use marked crosswalks, use caution at junctions, and be aware of your surroundings.

- Personal Protection: While Taiwan is largely secure, use common sense, particularly in congested locations. Maintain vigilance over your valuables, avoid publicly exhibiting precious objects, and use anti-theft methods such as money belts.

- Language Difficulties: Despite the fact that many residents understand English, there may be instances of language problems. It might be beneficial to learn a few basic Mandarin phrases, and translation applications can assist with communication.

Health Precautions

Let's look at some important health measures to keep you feeling your best while visiting this fascinating island.

Water and Food Safety

- Select Reliable Businesses: Taiwan is well-known for its diversified and delectable street cuisine. Choose vendors with clean and well-maintained booths to ensure food safety. Food booths that are popular and bustling frequently imply both quality and freshness.

- Hygiene Habits: Examine food handlers' cleanliness habits. Look for vendors that wear gloves, clean their

© John D. Travelar

utensils on a regular basis, and demonstrate a dedication to cleanliness. Freshly made meals are often safer than pre-packaged ones.

- Consume Bottled Water: While tap water is typically safe in Taiwan, many residents and visitors prefer bottled water. Carry a reusable water bottle filled with bottled or filtered water to remain hydrated, particularly in the humid environment.

Sun and Heat Defense

- The sun in Taiwan may be harsh, especially during the summer months. Use sunscreen with a high SPF, wear sunglasses, and a wide-brimmed hat to protect your skin. Long-sleeved, lightweight garments may also give extra protection.

- Hydration: Staying hydrated is critical in hot and humid conditions. Drink lots of water throughout the day, particularly if you're doing anything outside. Consider bringing a refillable water bottle to lessen your environmental effect.

Insect Defence

- Use an insect repellent: Mosquitoes may be common in some areas and at certain seasons. Use insect repellent to protect yourself from mosquito-borne infections. Apply it to exposed skin and clothes, particularly while participating in outdoor activities.

© John D. Travelar

- Long-sleeved shirts and pants: If you're going to be in an insect-infested location, consider wearing long sleeves and trousers. This adds another layer of defence against mosquito bites, ticks, and other potentially troublesome insects.

Medical Care and Medication

- Travel Insurance: Make sure you have adequate travel insurance that covers medical expenditures and emergency evacuation before you go. This gives you peace of mind in the event of an unforeseen health crisis.

- Keep Prescription Medications on Hand: Carry a sufficient supply of prescription pills in their original container if you take them. Also, have a list of generic names handy since brand names might fluctuate depending on where you live.

- Find Local Hospitals or Clinics: When you arrive, look for local hospitals or clinics in the places you want to visit. Because many medical personnel in Taiwan know English, communication is easier.

Overall Health

- Get Enough Sleep: Travelling may be thrilling, but it is important to prioritise relaxation. Make sure you get enough sleep to keep your immune system robust and your general health in check.

164

© John D. Travelar

- Maintain Physical Activity: Exploration combined with physical exercise benefits overall health. Taiwan has stunning scenery for hiking, walking, and other outdoor activities. In order to remain active, include exercise into your everyday routine.

- Disclose Dietary Restrictions: Communicate your dietary limitations or allergies explicitly, particularly when sampling new foods. Many Taiwanese folks are kind and would appreciate your efforts to make eating safe.

FAQs

- 1. Is street food safe to consume in Taiwan? Yes, Taiwanese street food is typically safe and a delectable gastronomic experience. Choose vendors with clean and bustling booths, exercise good hygiene, and enjoy a variety of delectable goods.

- 2. Do I need any immunizations before visiting Taiwan? Taiwan has no specified entrance vaccination requirements. However, it is important that you keep up with normal vaccines and check with your healthcare professional for any necessary immunizations depending on your travel plans.

- 3. What should I do if I have health problems during my trip? If you are experiencing health problems, get treatment at a local hospital or clinic. In an emergency, contact 119 to get an ambulance. For

© John D. Travelar

peace of mind, having comprehensive travel insurance that covers medical expenditures and evacuation is crucial.

- 4. Can I find over-the-counter drugs at Taiwan pharmacies? Yes, pharmacies (, yào j) are widespread in Taiwan. Pharmacists may help with minor illnesses and sell over-the-counter drugs. Carry any prescription pills you need in their original packaging.

- 5. Are there any unique health dangers in Taiwan around the typhoon season? During the typhoon season (June to October), threats include excessive rainfall and the likelihood of typhoons. Keep up with weather updates, obey any advisories or evacuation orders, and exercise caution in regions prone to floods or landslides.

Local Customs to Respect

Understanding and respecting local customs is the key to meaningful interactions and a culturally diverse experience as you begin on a tour to Taiwan, a nation where old traditions coexist with contemporary energy. Taiwan's rich cultural tapestry is intertwined with traditions that represent the island's history, values, and hospitality. Let's have a look at some important local traditions to embrace and respect throughout your stay.

© John D. Travelar

Greetings and Courtesy

- **Nodding and Bowing**: While handshakes are prevalent in professional settings, a traditional and courteous welcome is a nod or a modest bow. The depth of the bow may vary depending on formality and familiarity.

- **Addressing Others**: When addressing others, use titles and last names, particularly in formal contexts. It's a display of deference. Individuals may encourage you to use their given name after establishing a degree of familiarity.

Temples and Religious Structures

- **Entering Temples**: It is traditional to walk over the threshold rather than on it while entering a temple. This symbolic gesture expresses reverence for the holy location.

- **Temple Attire:** Dress modestly while visiting temples. Shorts, sleeveless shirts, and exposing apparel should be avoided. It is polite to cover your shoulders and knees.

- **Taking photographs**: Check for signs or seek permission before taking photographs inside a temple. Some temples may forbid photography or impose strict guidelines.

167

© John D. Travelar

Tea Etiquette and Culture

- **Accepting Tea**: It is polite to take tea when given. To express thanks, hold the tea cup with both hands. When accepting tea, a little nod or bow is usual.

- **Pouring Tea for Others:** If you observe someone's tea cup is empty, offer to fill it. This act is regarded as meaningful and demonstrates a feeling of community.

- **Tapping the Table:** Tapping the table with your fingertips expresses gratitude to the person serving tea. It's a nonverbal way of stating you've had your fill.

Gift-Giving Traditions

- **Offering Gifts**: Use both hands while offering a gift. Before receiving a gift, the receiver may deny it out of courtesy.

- **Opening Presents**: Gifts are often unwrapped in privacy. By insisting on opening the present in your presence, you avoid putting the receiver on the spot.

- **Red Envelopes (Hongbao):** During festivities, red envelopes are often utilised for monetary presents. The quantity of money should be representative of good fortune, with even numbers desirable.

© John D. Travelar

Etiquette for Dining

- sitting Arrangements: In formal situations, sitting may be allotted according to rank or age. Before taking your seat, wait for instructions.

- Using Chopsticks: Using chopsticks upright in a bowl of rice recalls a funeral ceremony. Place them horizontally or on a designated resting place.

First, Declining Food: As a courtesy, it is traditional to refuse food or beverages when given. It is likely, however, to accept a second offer.

Taiwanese culture is profoundly ingrained in its conventions and traditions. By adopting and honouring these practices, you not only demonstrate respect for the local way of life, but you also open the door to real experiences and relationships. Whether you're visiting temples, attending tea ceremonies, or attending celebratory parties, these practices offer layers of significance to your trip to Taiwan.

© John D. Travelar

SUSTAINABLE TRAVEL IN TAIWAN

The notion of sustainable travel is becoming more important as worldwide awareness of environmental challenges rises. Taiwan, with its beautiful landscapes, rich cultural history, and forward-thinking people, provides a great backdrop for adopting sustainable travel habits. Let's look at how you may tread gently and positively contribute to Taiwan's gorgeous island while having a pleasant and eco-conscious holiday experience.

Eco-Friendly Initiatives

Taiwan has emerged as a paragon of eco-friendly projects, thanks to its magnificent landscapes and devotion to environmental protection. The island is making major

© John D. Travelar

progress toward a greener and more sustainable future, from sustainable energy techniques to community-led conservation programs. Let's take a look at some of the incredible eco-friendly efforts that are transforming Taiwan's natural landscape.

Leadership in Renewable Energy

- Wind Power Development: Taiwan has established itself as a pioneer in offshore wind power. The government's dedication to renewable energy has resulted in the construction of wind farms along the shore, which use the island's rich wind resources to generate clean power.

- Solar Energy Expansion: Another important project is the promotion of solar energy. Solar panel installation on residential and commercial buildings has been promoted by government incentives, contributing to the country's renewable energy targets.

Effective Waste Management

- Waste-to-Energy Plants: Taiwan has invested in waste-to-energy plants that turn municipal solid waste into electricity. This method not only reduces landfill waste but also creates power, creating a circular economy.

- Recycling systems: Strict recycling systems are in existence, encouraging individuals to segregate their trash into several categories. High recycling rates

© John D. Travelar

have resulted from the government's initiatives, demonstrating the efficacy of citizen engagement in sustainable waste management.

Urban Greening Initiatives

- Green Roofs and Walls: Green roofs and walls are becoming more popular in Taiwanese cities. These programs promote urban biodiversity, air quality, and insulation, all of which contribute to more sustainable and livable cities.

Tree Planting efforts: Tree planting efforts conducted by communities attempt to improve green space in cities. These projects not only address urban heat islands but also encourage community participation in environmental protection.

Community-Based Conservation

- Coastal cleaning Initiatives: There are several coastal cleaning activities conducted by local communities and environmental groups. These programs aim to remove marine waste, raise awareness about ocean conservation, and protect Taiwan's beautiful coasts.

- Ecotourism Development: Promoting ecotourism coincides with the aims of sustainable development. Local communities are actively engaged in promoting their areas' natural beauty while stressing ethical and low-impact tourist methods.

172

© John D. Travelar

Programs for Environmental Education

- Green Curriculum in Schools: Taiwan has included environmental education into school curriculum, instilling a feeling of environmental responsibility in students from an early age. Students take part in environmentally responsible initiatives, forming a generation dedicated to sustainability.

- Government-Led Public Awareness Campaigns: emphasise the need of environmental conservation. These programs educate individuals on sustainable practices, energy conservation, and the environmental effect of individual acts.

Taiwan's dedication to environmentally friendly activities spans several areas, demonstrating a balanced marriage of environmental awareness with technical innovation. As these programs gain traction, Taiwan demonstrates the beneficial influence that proactive environmental stewardship may have on a nation's present and future.

Responsible Tourism Practices

As Taiwan entices visitors from all over the world, the need for ethical tourism practices cannot be stressed. Visitors may positively contribute to the island's natural and cultural assets by adopting sustainable and courteous travel practices. Let's take a look at a guide to ethical tourist practices that balance discovery and preservation.

© John D. Travelar

Respect Local Culture and Customs

- Cultural Awareness: Learn about the local traditions and cultural practices. When visiting religious sites, attending festivals, or engaging with local populations, show respect. Understanding and understanding cultural differences improves the whole travel experience.

- Learn simple words: Learning a few simple Mandarin words, like hello and thank you, shows a genuine interest in the local culture. Locals enjoy the effort, which fosters healthy relationships.

Aid Local Businesses and Communities

- Select Local lodgings: Choose locally owned lodgings such as boutique hotels, guesthouses, or homestays. This guarantees that a substantial amount of your investment directly helps the local community.

- Dine Locally: Sample traditional Taiwanese food at local cafes and marketplaces. Supporting local eateries not only provides a sense of the area but also helps small business owners make a living.

Reduce Environmental Impact

- Take Public Transportation: Taiwan has a well-developed public transportation system. Use trains, buses, and the MRT to explore the city and travel between cities. This cuts carbon emissions while also reducing traffic congestion.

© John D. Travelar

- Exercise Responsible Hiking: Stick to established pathways while trekking in Taiwan's magnificent landscapes to prevent damaging native ecosystems. Keep garbage to a minimum, keep on indicated pathways, and preserve animal habitats.

Reduce Your Use of Plastic

- Always Carry a Reusable Water Bottle: The tap water in Taiwan is safe to drink. Carrying a reusable water bottle helps to reduce plastic waste. Many public places and hotels include water refill facilities.

- Refuse Single-Use Plastics: Refuse single-use plastics such as straws and utensils politely. Bring your reusable alternatives to help reduce plastic pollution.

Help with Conservation Efforts

- Take Part in Cleanup Activities: Join local community-led cleanup efforts. Whether it's coastline cleaning or trail maintenance, actively engaging in conservation initiatives aids in the preservation of Taiwan's natural beauty.

- Support Wildlife Sanctuaries: If you want to see wildlife, pick sanctuaries that are well-managed and promote animal care. Activities that entail direct interaction with animals should be avoided.

Responsible tourism in Taiwan entails travelling with awareness and consideration. Visitors who adopt these

© John D. Travelar

behaviours not only have a more immersive and genuine experience, but they also help to preserve the island's natural marvels and cultural traditions. Taiwan welcomes visitors with the expectation that their experiences will be beneficial and long-lasting.

Supporting Local Communities

Travelling is about more than just seeing new places; it's about engaging with local cultures and communities. Supporting local communities enriches your vacation experience in Taiwan, a place with various customs and great welcome. Let's have a look at ways to empower and elevate the communities you come across on your trip in Taiwan.

Select Locally Owned Accommodations

- Boutique Hotels and Homestays: Choose locally owned and run boutique hotels, homestays, or guesthouses. These lodgings provide a personal and unique experience while directly contributing to the income of the local hosts.

- Community-Based Lodgings: Look into community-based accommodation choices where your stay directly helps the community. These programs often use revenue-sharing structures, guaranteeing that a percentage of your contribution is reinvested in community development.

Support Local Artists and Farmers Markets

© John D. Travelar

- handcrafted Crafts and Artwork: Look for local artists and craftsmen who make one-of-a-kind handcrafted things. Purchase items directly from these craftspeople to strengthen your connection to the local art scene and to support traditional workmanship.

- Explore Local Markets: Go to local markets to learn about regional specialties and engage with merchants. Your purchases directly benefit these small companies' lives, encouraging economic sustainability.

Take Part in Cultural Experiences

- Guided Tours by Locals: Choose guided tours offered by locals. This not only gives you an insider's view of the area, but it also assures that your tourist money goes directly to people in the neighbourhood.

- Cultural Workshops: Participate in cultural workshops and activities led by locals. Learning traditional skills, preparing regional cuisine, or participating in local events all foster important ties and contribute to cultural preservation.

Select Responsible Tourism Providers

- Eco-Friendly and Responsible Tours: Choose tour operators that are devoted to responsible and sustainable tourism. These businesses place a premium on reducing environmental effects, supporting local communities, and creating genuine experiences.

177

© John D. Travelar

- Community-Based Ecotourism: Investigate community-based ecotourism programs that enable you to interact responsibly and meaningfully with local communities. Home visits, cultural performances, and joint conservation efforts are often included in these projects.

Respect for Local Environments and Traditions

- Leave No Trace: Practise responsible tourism by leaving natural areas in the same condition in which you found them. Reduce your ecological impact, prevent trash, and stick to authorised trails while engaging in outdoor activities.

- Respect Cultural Norms: Become acquainted with and respect local cultural norms. This involves following clothing requirements, acting appropriately in religious settings, and knowing traditional practices. This guarantees that interactions with the local community are amicable.

Supporting local communities in Taiwan entails more than just monetary donations; it also entails making true relationships and having a good impression. You may help strengthen communities by staying in locally owned hotels, connecting with local craftspeople, participating in cultural activities, supporting responsible tourism operators, and preserving both the environment and cultural customs. Your

© **John D. Travelar**

trip becomes a joint effort to preserve and celebrate the many cultures of Taiwan.

© John D. Travelar

PRACTICAL TIPS

Travelling to Taiwan promises to be an adventure full of cultural diversity, magnificent scenery, and lively experiences. To guarantee a smooth and happy travel experience, be well-prepared and familiar with practical advice that can enrich your stay. Let's get started with a detailed guide to touring Taiwan with ease.

Tipping Etiquette

Tipping etiquette can be a tricky business while travelling, and Taiwan is no different. While tipping is not as common in Taiwanese society as it is in certain Western nations, learning the intricacies might help you have a better cultural experience. Let's take a look at tipping in Taiwan, where appreciation is shown via gestures rather than monetary donations.

© John D. Travelar

Restaurants and Cafés

- Service Charges Included: Many premium restaurants and hotels levy a service fee, which is generally approximately 10% of the cost. Additional tipping is not anticipated in such circumstances. Before adding a tip, double-check the bill for the service fee.

- Local Restaurants and Street Food: Tipping is not widespread practice at local restaurants and street food booths. Small change or rounding up the bill, on the other hand, is welcomed. If you get great service, a token of appreciation is appropriate.

Taxis and Transportation

- Taxis: It is not common to tip taxi drivers. Simply round up to the closest suitable quantity. Giving NT$200, for example, if the fare is NT$180, is a courteous way to demonstrate thanks.

- Public transit: Tipping is not required for public transit, including buses and the MRT (Mass Rapid Transit). The approach works well, and appreciation is more often shown via courteous conduct.

Hotels & Lodging

- Service workers: Although bellhops and cleaning workers do not demand gratuities, a little tip for exemplary service is appreciated. It is considered courteous to provide between NT$50 and NT$100.

© John D. Travelar

- Concierge Services: A little tip is a nice gesture if the concierge goes above and beyond to help you. For their efforts, NT$100 to NT$200 is a reasonable compensation.

Spa and Wellness Facilities

- Spa and Massage Services: Tipping for spa and massage services is appreciated at businesses that do not include a service fee. For exceptional service, a tip of 10% to 15% of the service fee is usual.

Guided Tours & Excursions

- Group Tours: Check to see whether a service fee is included in group tours, particularly those arranged by tour firms. If not, a daily tip of NT$200 to NT$300 for the guide is a kind gesture.

- Private Guides: Depending on the duration and intricacy of the trip, a larger tip of NT$500 to NT$1,000 is recommended for private guides.

Tipping is not as deeply rooted in Taiwanese society as it is in other areas of the globe. While it is not always required, showing thanks via simple gestures like rounding up the amount is appreciated. Understanding and honouring local traditions contributes to a happy and culturally rewarding experience in Taiwan, where sincere gestures typically outnumber monetary gratuities.

© John D. Travelar

Internet and Connectivity

Staying connected is an important component of travel in the era of digital discovery. Taiwan, with its technologically advanced environment, provides travellers with great internet and connection possibilities. This guide will help you get the most of your connection experience in Taiwan, whether you're traversing the hectic streets of Taipei or visiting the picturesque splendor of the countryside.

SIM Cards and Mobile Phone Plans

- Affordable Purchase Options: SIM cards with data plans are widely accessible at airports, convenience stores, and mobile carrier stores. Select a package that meets your data requirements for the length of your stay.

- Popular providers: Chunghwa Telecom, Taiwan Mobile, and FarEasTone are among Taiwan's leading mobile providers. Comparing their services can help you pick the finest coverage and data bundles for your needs.

Portable Wireless Network Devices

- Portable Wi-Fi Rental: Consider hiring a portable Wi-Fi device for consistent connection. These devices give a safe and dependable internet connection for many devices and may be picked up at airports or delivered to your lodging.

183

- Coverage and Speed: Portable Wi-Fi devices provide extensive coverage in both urban and rural locations. Taiwan's 4G network offers fast and steady internet connections, enabling you to browse maps, keep in contact, and share your trip experiences with ease.

Wi-Fi Hotspots in Public

- Citywide Protection: Many Taiwanese cities, particularly Taipei, have public Wi-Fi hotspots in public places, transit hubs, and tourism destinations. These hotspots provide free internet connectivity for limited periods of time.

How to Connect to Public Wi-Fi Select the network and follow the on-screen directions to connect to public Wi-Fi. Some networks may ask you to register using a local phone number.

Internet Cafés

- Urban Hubs: Internet cafés, sometimes known as "mangas," are ubiquitous in cities. These cafés provide computer access as well as high-speed internet. They are great for business travellers who want a separate office or gamers searching for a one-of-a-kind experience.

- Hourly Rates: Internet cafes normally charge by the hour. While keeping connected to friends, family, or business, enjoy a relaxing setting with refreshments and drinks.

© John D. Travelar

Connectivity to Hotels and Other Accommodations

- Wi-Fi Availability: Most hotels and motels in Taiwan provide free Wi-Fi to its customers. When reserving your stay, confirm the availability of Wi-Fi and ask about any access credentials or limitations.

- Business Centers: If you want extra connection services, hotels often feature business centres with PCs, printers, and high-speed internet for guest use.

Taiwan's dedication to technical improvements guarantees that tourists may remain connected in a smooth and easy manner.

Transportation Etiquette

Taiwanese society values efficient and courteous transportation. Understanding and abiding to transit etiquette will improve your vacation experience as you enjoy the busy cities and quiet surroundings. Let's explore the complexities of navigating elegantly across Taiwan's diversified transportation network, from public transportation to taxis.

Mass Rapid Transit (MRT) Etiquette

- Queuing System: Observe the queueing system while waiting for the MRT. Allow passengers to disembark the train before standing in line. This method guarantees that passengers move smoothly and orderly.

© John D. Travelar

- Reserved Seats: In MRT vehicles, priority seats are reserved for senior passengers, pregnant women, and those with impairments. If you take these seats, be ready to give them up to others who need them more.

Bus Etiquette
- Enter and Exit Gracefully: Before boarding a bus, wait for people to exit. Move to the back to create room for others. Exit the bus as soon as possible, enabling people behind you to alight easily.

- Providing Seats: Buses, like the MRT, offer dedicated seats for customers with special needs. Be kind and provide these seats to people in need.

Etiquette in Taxis
- Line Up at Taxi Stands: Whenever feasible, utilise authorised taxi stands when hailing a cab. Stopping taxis in the middle of the road might cause traffic congestion.

- Use Hand Gestures: While taxis have meters, it's easier to indicate your destination using hand gestures or a basic map. This provides clarity and a more pleasant travel.

Bike Etiquette
- Remain in Designated Lanes: Taiwan is a bike-friendly country, with dedicated bike lanes in several cities. To protect your safety and the safety of pedestrians, stay in these designated lanes.

© John D. Travelar

- Follow Traffic Signals: When bicycling, obey traffic signals and laws. Stopping at red lights and yielding to pedestrians are examples of this. Helmets are advised for safety.

Walking Manners
- Walk on the Right: In congested locations such as train stations and busy streets, follow the unwritten norm of walking on the right side. This contributes to the smooth flow of pedestrian traffic.

Avoid Blocking Pathways: If you need to check your phone or review a map, move aside to allow pedestrian traffic to pass. In congested regions, this civility is much appreciated.

Training Etiquette
- Seat Reservations: If you have a seat reservation on a train, please take it. If not, choose an open seat and be prepared to abandon it if the proper person comes.

- Silent carriages: Certain rail carriages are labelled as "quiet cars." Maintain a modest conversation level and refrain from using electronic devices without headphones in these specified places.

Understanding and following Taiwanese transportation etiquette is essential for a pleasant travel experience. Whether you're using the efficient MRT system, taking buses, calling cabs, bicycling, or just strolling through bustling streets, being polite adds to Taiwan's overall transportation harmony.

187

© John D. Travelar

FAQs

1. Is there a set of laws in Taiwan for using electronic devices on public transportation? While there are no hard and fast restrictions, using headphones while listening to music or viewing movies on public transit is considered respectful. Keep the volume down to prevent disturbing other passengers.

2. Can I ride my bike on Taiwanese public transportation? Folding bikes are permitted at several MRT stations and trains. During busy hours, however, ordinary motorcycles may be restricted. Inquire with station officials or train attendants about carrying bikes on public transit.

3. Is it customary in Taiwan to tip taxi drivers? Tipping is not common in Taiwan, and this includes taxi drivers. It is appreciated if the fare is simply rounded up to the next convenient amount. Taxi drivers are used to this routine.

4. Can I eat or drink on Taiwanese public transportation? when it is not expressly forbidden, it is generally courteous to avoid eating strong-smelling meals when on public transit. Keep an eye on the environment's cleanliness and properly dispose of any rubbish.

5. Are there dedicated stroller places on public transportation? Yes, there are specific stroller spots on many buses and MRT vehicles. Fold strollers whenever feasible to conserve room and provide a more comfortable ride for other passengers.

© John D. Travelar

SHOPPING IN TAIWAN

Taiwan is a sanctuary for consumers looking for a diversified retail experience, with its colourful markets, sophisticated shopping areas, and traditional artisan stores. This tour will take you across Taiwan's shopping scene, from stylish shops to hectic night markets, ensuring you discover the greatest treasures the island has to offer.

Modern Marvel
- Ximending: Visit Ximending in Taipei for a sample of contemporary shopping. This stylish neighbourhood is a hotspot for teenage culture and fashion. Discover the eclectic mix of boutiques, foreign brands, and eccentric businesses that line the busy streets.

- The Taipei 101 Mall, located inside the landmark Taipei 101 building, has premium brands, designer

© John D. Travelar

retailers, and high-end boutiques. For those looking for top-tier items, this refined shopping centre offers a premium experience.

Traditional Crafts and Artisanal Discoveries

- Dihua Street: Located in Taipei, Dihua Street is a treasure trove of traditional Taiwanese items. This ancient street is a mix of old and contemporary, selling anything from medicinal plants to dry products. Explore traditional tea shops, antique apothecaries, and specialty spice shops.

- Jiufen Old Street: Perched on a hill overlooking the seaside, the tiny Jiufen Old Street is known for its nostalgic charm and artisanal businesses. In this gorgeous environment, you may find handmade products, traditional teas, and delicate pottery.

Specialty Markets

- Taipei Jade Market: Explore the cultural importance of jade art Taipei's Jade Market. This market has a wide range of jade items, from jewellery to exquisite sculptures. Learn about the many varieties of jade and choose a piece that speaks to you.

Taichung Flower and Jade Market: The Flower and Jade Market in Taichung is a mix of nature and artistry. Discover magnificent jade artefacts while exploring shops decked with bright flowers. The market offers a delectable combination of floral beauty and artisanal expertise.

Tainan Boutique Shopping

- Shennong Street: Shennong Street in Tainan, Taiwan's oldest city, provides one-of-a-kind retail experiences. Explore boutique stores in old buildings that feature local arts, crafts, and traditional delicacies. The vintage atmosphere of the street adds to the allure of your shopping excursion.

- Hayashi Department Store: Immerse yourself in the magnificence of Tainan's Hayashi Department Store. This ancient enterprise, which dates back to the Japanese colonial period, is a luxury shopping destination. Browse through worldwide and local products in a historical atmosphere.

Night Markets and Local Bazaars

Taiwan's bustling night markets and small bazaars come to life as the sun sets and the cityscape lights up. These midnight

© John D. Travelar

hotspots provide a kaleidoscope of aromas, sights, and sounds, resulting in an immersive experience for both residents and tourists. Join us on an intriguing tour through Taiwan's night markets and bazaars, where every booth has a tale to tell.

Taipei's Shilin Night Market

Street Food Galore: Shilin Night Market in Taipei is a gourmet feast that draws foodies from all over the world. Enjoy traditional Taiwanese street dishes such as stinky tofu, oyster omelettes, and bubble tea. The combination of tastes and textures creates a gastronomic symphony that tempts the taste receptors.

Fashion and Accessories: Shilin has a variety of fashion booths and trinket stores in addition to the delightful fragrances. The market shows the newest trends in Taiwanese fashion, from stylish apparel to eccentric accessories. In the vibrant setting, bargain seekers may polish their abilities.

Taipei's Raohe Street Night Market

Historic Charm: Nestled in the centre of Taipei, Raohe Street Night Market emanates historic charm. The lovely mood is created by the landmark entry gate, Ciyou Temple, and traditional Chinese architecture. Discover hidden jewels while strolling through the small pathways decked with crimson lamps.

Antiques and Crafts: Raohe is well-known for its antique stores and market booths selling traditional goods. Investigate elaborately carved wooden objects, calligraphy brushes, and

© John D. Travelar

handcrafted jewellery. The market is a treasure mine for people looking for one-of-a-kind gifts with a Taiwanese flair.

Pingtung's Kenting Night Market

Extravagant Seafood Buffet: This night market in the southern seaside town of Kenting is a seafood lover's dream. Delectable meals are created with fresh fish from neighbouring seas. The market encapsulates the flavour of seaside life, from grilled squid to seafood hot pots.

Local Art and Performances: Kenting Night Market is more than simply a food market; it's also a cultural show. Local artists often perform traditional music and dance, giving a vibrant element to the evening. Visitors may immerse themselves in the region's creative offerings.

Kaohsiung's Liuhe Tourist Night Market

Foodie Mecca: Liuhe Tourist Night Market in Kaohsiung is a foodie's paradise for real Taiwanese cuisine. Try grilled mochi, coffin bread, and enormous sausages, among other local favourites. The market's varied culinary options reflect Taiwan's rich gourmet tradition.

Souvenirs & trinkets: While enjoying the gastronomic pleasures, peruse the shops offering souvenirs and trinkets. During keychains to handcrafted goods, Liuhe Market is a great spot to pick up souvenirs during your trip to Kaohsiung.

Local Bazaars

Taipei's Dihua Street: Historical Enclave: Dihua Street is a historical enclave in the centre of Taipei that comes to life

193

© John D. Travelar

during local bazaars. Investigate traditional medicine shops, tea establishments, and dry goods businesses. The timeless appeal of the street offers a look into Taiwan's rich past.

Tainan's Jingzaijiao Tile-Paved Salt Fields: Salty Souvenirs: The Jingzaijiao Tile-Paved Salt Fields in Tainan host local bazaars where tourists may buy unique salt-related goods. These bazaars highlight the region's salt producing tradition by selling everything from handcrafted salted delicacies to bath salts.

Taiwanese Souvenirs

Bringing home a piece of Taiwan is more than simply buying something; it's about capturing the spirit of the island's rich culture, history, and workmanship. Taiwanese souvenirs range from tasty snacks to handmade artefacts and represent the island's unique traditions. Let's take a stroll into the fascinating world of genuine Taiwanese souvenirs.

Pineapple Cakes

Ancient Taiwanese Delight: Pineapple cakes are a traditional Taiwanese dessert and a favourite souvenir. The sweet and acidic pineapple interior is enclosed in a flaky crust of these bite-sized pastries. They come in nicely designed gift boxes and make excellent presents for friends and family.

Recommended Brands: Look for well-known brands such as Chia Te Bakery and SunnyHills, which are recognized for producing high-quality pineapple cakes. These products often use local ingredients, delivering a genuine and delightful experience.

Oolong Tea

Heritage of Tea: Taiwan is famous for its Oolong tea, and taking home a bag of this fragrant and tasty tea is a lovely way to immerse yourself in the island's tea culture. Oolong tea comes in a variety of flavours, each with its own distinct flavour character.

Tea Gift packages: Purchase Oolong tea gift packages, which include neatly wrapped tea leaves and traditional teaware. These sets not only display the excellence of Taiwanese tea, but they also make for visually appealing gifts.

Hand-Painted Ceramics

Ceramics in Jingdezhen Style: Ceramics have a long history in Taiwan, and hand-painted objects showcase the island's creative legacy. Look for Jingdezhen-style pottery with elaborate motifs and bright hues. These objects, ranging from teapots to beautiful dishes, offer a sense of beauty to any household.

Night Market Finds: Look for one-of-a-kind, hand-painted ceramic items produced by individual craftsmen at local markets and night markets. These one-of-a-kind objects exemplify Taiwanese craftsmanship's ingenuity and distinctiveness.

Timeless Elegance

© John D. Travelar

Artistic Expression: Chinese calligraphy is an important part of Taiwanese culture. Traditional calligraphy brushes are excellent gifts when created with accuracy and care. These brushes are often accompanied with ink sticks and ink stones, completing the ensemble for creative expression.

Artisan Workshops: Observe the workmanship behind these calligraphy brushes at artisan workshops. Some workshops even provide bespoke brushes, letting you choose the handle and bristle materials for a really one-of-a-kind keepsake.

Formosan Aboriginal Crafts

Indigenous Artistry: Immerse yourself in Taiwan's indigenous culture by purchasing traditional items made by the island's aboriginal populations. Handwoven fabrics, beading, and wood sculptures demonstrate Formosan tribes' craftsmanship and cultural value.

Fair Trade Products: Encourage fair trade groups to work with indigenous craftsmen. By purchasing these items, you are helping to preserve traditional artistry and the economic well-being of indigenous communities.

Bargaining Tips

In Taiwan, bargaining is more than simply a transaction; it's a cultural dance, a convivial interaction that adds flavour to the shopping experience. Bargaining is a skill worth developing, from hectic night markets to modest street vendors. Let's get

196

started on negotiating costs and getting the most of your Taiwan shopping trip.

Take a Friendly Approach

Smile and Interact: Start with a grin. Approach negotiation as a friendly rather than a competitive relationship. Starting the discussion with a friendly welcome develops a favourable tone and a relationship with the seller.

A Little Politeness Can Go a Long Way: In Taiwanese culture, politeness is essential. Maintain a nice tone and courteous words during the discussion. Being nice and polite may often lead to better offers.

Understand the Market Value

Do Your Research Beforehand: Become acquainted with the overall market worth of the item in question. This information serves as your starting point for negotiations. It keeps you from overpaying and gives you a good starting point for talks.

Ask Locals for Insights: Engage in polite interactions with locals to learn about fair pricing. They may provide useful information about what to anticipate and maybe discuss some negotiation strategies utilised in the region.

Begin with a Counteroffer

courteous Counter Offers: After the original price is mentioned, make a courteous counteroffer that is a little lower than what you are ready to spend. This opens the door for bargaining and enables both sides to strive toward a mutually acceptable price.

© John D. Travelar

Incorporate Hand movements: Use hand movements to indicate your counteroffer. Nonverbal communication may be a very effective strategy, particularly when there is a language barrier. A little downward movement of the hand may indicate a lesser price.

Learn the Art of Walking Away

Strategic Retreat: Be prepared to walk away if the merchant does not meet your targeted pricing. This is a frequent negotiation strategy. It indicates to the merchant that you are prepared to forego the purchase until a better price is given.

encourage the seller to rethink: As you move away from the item, indicate your interest in it and encourage the seller to rethink their pricing. This subtle act of leaving the bargaining table may often lead the seller to make a more tempting offer.

Bundle Items for Better Prices

Bundle Purchases: Consider combining several goods at a lower price. When it comes to selling more things in a single transaction, vendors are frequently more inclined to lower the total price. This strategy works especially well in marketplaces with a variety of vendors.

Express real Interest: Show real enthusiasm for the products you're combining. Customers who enjoy their items are valued by vendors. This may result in lower cost for the combined product.

© **John D. Travelar**

Bargaining is a participatory and joyful part of the shopping experience in Taiwan. You may master the art of negotiating by adopting a pleasant attitude, recognizing the market value, and applying effective negotiation strategies. Remember, it's not just about the final price; it's about the shared experience of striking a bargain in Taiwan's vibrant marketplaces.

CONCLUSION

Imagine the beautiful landscapes, rich cultural tapestry, and warm hospitality that await you on the intriguing island as you approach the final pages of our Taiwan travel guide. Taiwan, with its numerous attractions, is more than just a destination; it's a tapestry of experiences waiting to be discovered.

Recap of Essential Travel Tips

As you prepare to go to Taiwan, it is critical to arm yourself with practical information to guarantee a pleasant and rewarding travel experience. Let's go over some of the fundamental travel recommendations that will help you navigate this enthralling island's vivid landscapes, cultural treasures, and gastronomic pleasures.

© John D. Travelar

Visa Prerequisites: Check Taiwan's visa requirements for your nationality before packing your luggage. Check that your passport is valid for at least six months after your intended travel date. Depending on your place of origin, you may be eligible for visa-free entrance or need a visa ahead of time.

Best Time to Visit: Taiwan has four different seasons, each with its own particular beauty. When arranging your vacation, keep the weather and your favoured activities in mind. Spring (March to May) and fall (September to November) include warm weather and flowering sceneries.

Money and Currency Advice: The New Taiwan Dollar (TWD) is the national currency. Learn about current exchange rates and consider withdrawing cash from ATMs for local purchases, particularly in marketplaces and smaller restaurants where credit cards may not be readily accepted.

How to Get There: Taiwan has international airports at Taipei, Taoyuan, and Kaohsiung, and is well-connected by air. Based on your departure location, look for direct flights or convenient layovers. Consider pre-booking transportation from the airport to your lodging for a stress-free arrival.

Internal Taiwan Transportation: The island has an excellent and easily accessible transportation system. In big cities, high-speed trains, buses, and the MRT (Mass Rapid Transit) make moving around easy. Purchase transit passes to travel across areas in a cost-effective and smooth manner.

© John D. Travelar

Language and Communication Hints: While Mandarin Chinese is the official language, many inhabitants, particularly in metropolitan regions and tourist sites, also speak English. To improve your relationships, learn a few basic Mandarin words and utilise translation applications in less English-friendly places.

Accommodation: Plan ahead of time, particularly during high seasons. Taiwan has a variety of accommodations, ranging from luxury hotels to budget-friendly hostels and traditional guesthouses. Consider staying in a variety of lodgings to experience Taiwan's distinct hospitality.

Culinary Delights: Taiwanese food will be a highlight of your trip. Try street cuisine at night markets and enjoy regional delicacies to immerse yourself in the local dining culture. Don't be afraid to ask locals for ideas, and be open to trying tastes that are unfamiliar to you.

Health and Safety Recommendations: Travellers to Taiwan are typically safe. Take basic safety measures, be alert of your surroundings, and keep your possessions secure. Although Taiwan's healthcare system is good, it is recommended that you carry travel insurance that covers medical emergencies.

Responsible Tourism Practices: Respect local traditions, reduce trash, and support eco-friendly activities to contribute to sustainable and responsible tourism. Engage with local communities in culturally appropriate ways to make a good impression on the locations you visit.

© **John D. Travelar**

You'll be well-prepared to start on a fantastic tour in Taiwan if you keep these vital travel recommendations in mind. Let the island's charm and warmth capture you as you traverse its many attractions, whether you're visiting busy towns, tranquil landscapes, or savouring local specialties. Best wishes

ITINERARIES

Day 1 exploring TAIPEI

Time	Activity	Location	Cost
9:00 AM	Breakfast at a local tea house	Yong Kang Street	$20
10:30 AM	Visit Chiang Kai-shek Memorial Hall	Zhongzheng District	Free
1:00 PM	Lunch at Din Tai Fung (Xinyi Branch)	Xinyi District	$30
3:00 PM	Explore Taipei 101 and its surroundings	Xinyi District	$25
6:00 PM	Dinner at Addiction Aquatic	Zhongshan District	$40

© John D. Travelar

	Development		
8:00 PM	Night market experience at Shilin	Shilin District	$15
10:00 PM	Return to hotel		

Day 2 Nature and Culture

Time	Activity	Location	Cost
8:00 AM	Breakfast at Fu Hang Soy Milk	Zhongzheng District	$15
9:30 AM	Day trip to Jiufen and Shifen Old Street	New Taipei City	$50
1:00 PM	Lunch overlooking the ocean	Jiufen	$20
3:00 PM	Visit Yehliu Geopark	Wanli District	$35
6:00 PM	Return to Taipei and freshen up		
8:00 PM	Dinner at Modern Toilet Restaurant	Ximending District	$35
10:00 PM	Night stroll at	Ximending	$10

© John D. Travelar

	Ximending Night Market	District	

Day 3: Cultural Immersion

Time	Activity	Location	Cost
9:00 AM	Visit National Palace Museum	Shilin District	$25
12:00 PM	Lunch at Din Tai Fung (again, it's a must!)	Zhongshan District	$30
2:00 PM	Explore Dihua Street	Datong District	$20
5:00 PM	Riverfront walk along Tamsui Old Street	Tamsui District	Free
7:00 PM	Dinner at Tamsui Fisherman's Wharf	Tamsui District	$40
9:00 PM	Sunset view at Lover's Bridge	Tamsui District	Free

Day 4: Southern Charm

Time	Activity	Location	Cost

© **John D. Travelar**

8:00 AM	Breakfast at Ah Zong Mian Xian	Ximending District	$15
9:30 AM	High-Speed Rail to Kaohsiung		$50
12:30 PM	Lunch at Liuhe Night Market	Xinxing District	$20
2:00 PM	Explore Fo Guang Shan Buddha Museum	Dashu District	$25
6:00 PM	Dinner at Cijin Seafood Street	Cijin District	$35
8:00 PM	Enjoy the Love River at night	Yancheng District	Free

Day 5: Adventure in Tainan

Time	Activity	Location	Cost
8:00 AM	Breakfast at Du Xiao Yue Danzi Noodle	West Central District	$15
9:30 AM	Visit Chihkan Tower and Fort Provintia	West Central District	$20
12:30 PM	Lunch at A-Shin Tainan	Anping District	$30

© John D. Travelar

	Tan-Tsu-Mien Seafood		
2:00 PM	Explore Koxinga Shrine and Anping Old Street	Anping District	Free
6:00 PM	Dinner at Shennong Street	North District	$35
8:00 PM	Night market at Flower Night Market	North District	$15

Day 6: Scenic East Coast

Time	Activity	Location	Cost
7:00 AM	Breakfast at a local café	Hualien City	$15
8:30 AM	Taroko Gorge National Park Adventure	Xiulin Township	$40
1:00 PM	Lunch in Taroko Village	Xiulin Township	$25
3:00 PM	Explore Qixingtan Scenic Area	Xincheng Township	Free
6:00 PM	Dinner at Hualien Dongdamen Night Market	Hualien City	$20

© John D. Travelar

Day 7: Farewell to Taiwan

Time	Activity	Location	Cost
9:00 AM	Visit Shuanglian Morning Market	Datong District	$20
11:00 AM	Brunch at Addiction Aquatic Development	Zhongshan District	$30
1:00 PM	Relaxing time at Daan Forest Park	Da'an District	Free
4:00 PM	Souvenir shopping at Taipei 101 Mall	Xinyi District	$50
7:00 PM	Dinner at Din Tai Fung (last time, promise!)	Xinyi District	$35
9:00 PM	Evening stroll at Elephant Mountain	Xinyi District	Free

Total Estimated Budget for Activities: $1,165

This comprehensive itinerary ensures you experience the best of Taiwan, from its vibrant city life to its breathtaking natural wonders and delicious cuisine. Enjoy your trip of a lifetime!

Made in United States
Troutdale, OR
01/05/2024

16719173R00116